INTERNATIONAL BANK FOR REÇONSTRUCTION AND DEVELOPMENT

WORLD BANK STAFF OCCASIONAL PAPERS NUMBER FIFTEEN

WORLD BANK STAFF OCCASIONAL PAPERS NUMBER FIFTEEN

Edited by

T. H. Silcock and Ian Bowen

ANTHONY CHURCHILL
in collaboration with Klaus Huber, Elke
Meldau and Alan Walters

ROAD USER CHARGES IN CENTRAL AMERICA

Distributed by The Johns Hopkins University Press
Baltimore and London

FOREWORD

I would like to explain *why* the World Bank Group does research work, and why it publishes it. We feel an obligation to look beyond the projects we help to finance toward the whole resource allocation of an economy, and the effectiveness of the use of those resources. Our major concern, in dealings with member countries, is that all scarce resources, including capital, skilled labor, enterprise and know-how, should be used to their best advantage. We want to see policies that encourage appropriate increases in the supply of savings, whether domestic or international. Finally, we are required by our Articles, as well as by inclination, to use objective economic criteria in all our judgments.

These are our preoccupations, and these, one way or another, are the subjects of most of our research work. Clearly, they are also the proper concern of anyone who is interested in promoting development, and so we seek to make our research papers widely available. In doing so, we have to take the risk of being misunderstood. Although these studies are published by the Bank, the views expressed and the methods explored should not necessarily be considered to represent the Bank's views or policies. Rather they are offered as a modest contribution to the great discussion on how to advance the economic development of the underdeveloped world.

ROBERT S. MCNAMARA
President
International Bank for
Reconstruction and Development

v

TABLE OF CONTENTS

PREFACE

The interest and controversy generated by the Bank's publication of A. A. Walters' *The Economics of Road User Charges* (World Bank Staff Occasional Paper No. 5) have led to this further exploration of the same topic. Our feeling was that the essentially theoretical nature of Walters' study should be confronted with the practical problems of the real world.

This paper is thus an application in Central America of the principles of pricing of road user services. Central America was selected for this case study as a result of the Bank's involvement in the financing of highways in this region and the willingness of the five governments concerned to extend their cooperation, without which this study would not have been possible. The recent establishment of the Central American Common Market made the topic very timely as each country sought to examine its own national system within the context of an increasingly unified market.

The authors have concluded that the principles and methods they have used do indeed provide useful insights into the problem of how to price the services provided by roads. The recommendations they have made are illustrative; they indicate the direction of change. Political, social and administrative factors may dictate a different solution. The framework of analysis developed in this paper is broad enough, however, to encompass the variety of goals that is part of any political and economic system. It is hoped that this study will be a useful example to policy-makers in this field of how to tackle the problems of road pricing.

The acceptance of the concepts advanced by the authors is by no means universal even within the Bank. The publication of this paper for wider circulation is an expression of our belief that only through a free communication of the ideas and results of our research will we be able to make a contribution to the advancement of the knowledge and understanding of the process of development.

This study was prepared during the latter half of 1967 and the early part of 1968 by the Bank Staff. The study team was headed by Anthony Churchill and consisted of Klaus Huber, Alan Walters (consultant), Jose Bronfman and Miss Elke Meldau. The authors wish to thank many of their colleagues in the Bank for their help and support. Particular thanks are due to Stanley Please, Alexander Stevenson, Mervyn Weiner, Vincent Hogg and Herman van der Tak who encouraged and supported this endeavor. Invaluable comments and help were also received from George Beier, Bernard Bell and Warren Baum. Special thanks must go to Professor William Vickrey who carefully read the manuscript and suggested many improvements. In addition the authors wish to acknowledge their debt to the many officials in the governments of Central America who enthusiastically cooperated in the work of this study. Finally the authors wish to thank Mrs. Maria del Solar who provided the secretarial assistance for the study team and who typed many of the drafts of the manuscript.

ANTHONY CHURCHILL

ROAD USER CHARGES IN CENTRAL AMERICA

I

SUMMARY

The World Bank has long been concerned with the pricing of road services, and commissioned Professor Alan Walters of the University of Birmingham to study the problem of road pricing. This study, which was completed early in 1967,[1] considered the economics of road pricing in a general context. It was recognized, however, that a case study would be required in order to examine the feasibility and implications of the theoretical analysis in a particular country. The choice of Central America for this purpose was coincidental with the operational needs of the Bank. During the negotiation of a loan for the paving of the Western Highway in Honduras, the question was raised as to what should be considered an adequate level of user charges. The Government of Honduras and the Bank agreed that the problem should be studied, particularly within the context of the rapidly developing Central American Common Market. The Bank further agreed to undertake such a study in cooperation with the governments of the member countries of the Common Market. This document is the result.

The primary goal of this study has been the achievement, to the maximum extent possible through the pricing of road services, of an efficient allocation of

---

[1] Alan Walters, *The Economics of Road User Charges*, World Bank Staff Occasional Paper Number 5 (Baltimore: The Johns Hopkins Press, 1968).

1

resources within the Common Market. The focus of the study is thus economic growth. Wider considerations such as the contribution of road taxes to public revenues or their role in redistributing income have been brought into the analysis. Each has been considered within the context of resource allocation. Goals often conflict; here it is the duty of the economist to point out the costs of the alternative paths open to the policy-maker.

The theoretical issues are briefly discussed in Chapter II. If the maximum net benefit from the highway network is to be achieved, the correct price to be charged users is a price equal to the cost of the resources used up when a journey is made. These resource costs consist of variable maintenance costs plus congestion costs—the costs that arise when a vehicle increases the costs of all other vehicles. Prices sufficient to cover these costs are defined by the study as the economic user charges. This price will provide the correct signals for the location of economic activity, and the use of the road network. It does not, however, provide information that is of much use for guiding road investment decisions, but this is inherent in any system of road pricing. Signals given by price or revenues cannot be substituted for the analysis of expected costs and benefits.

Financial constraints such as budgetary problems or a desire to tax road transport per se may require deviations from these prices. Such deviations should, however, be seen as responses to particular fiscal or administrative problems rather than as relating to the efficiency of the transport sector—though they should aim to reduce to a minimum any distortions to the transport sector.

In Chapter III the pricing of road services is placed within the context of the transportation system in Central America. In Chapter IV an attempt is made to estimate the variable maintenance costs generated by vehicles using uncongested highways, though the data available for this purpose leaves much to be desired. The best evidence available suggests that 0.1 US cents per vehicle kilometer is the cost caused by an average vehicle using a paved road. The costs are higher on unpaved roads, but because most of the vehicle kilometers take place on paved highways and because of the difficulty of designing a system of user charges to cover all types of road services, the study suggests that pricing policy be based on the use of paved roads. Available evidence also suggests that heavier vehicles cause higher costs.

Chapter V summarizes the current system of user charges in all Central American countries. All five countries have roughly similar levels of taxes, although the precise levels of individual taxes vary from country to country. The appropriateness of each tax as a user charge (i.e., for recovering the variable maintenance costs) as well as its possibilities as a revenue raising measure is examined. The cost of using the highway system is then contrasted with the actual charges levied (Chapter VI). The conclusion reached is that current charges are considerably in excess of the economic costs of using the uncongested highway network. On the average, current user charges raise the price of transport 20 percent above economic costs. It is estimated that the consequent loss of output is equal to between 0.2 and 2 percent of GDP, depending on the assumptions made; that is, GDP would be between 0.2 and 2 percent higher if the objective of road pricing policy were to charge only variable maintenance costs.

The problem of urban congestion is taken up in Chapter VII. The study shows that a high degree of congestion exists in all major Central American cities. Failure to reflect this congestion in the costs of using urban streets is rapidly leading to an intolerable situation. This is further aggravated by the poor financial situation of the major urban authorities and is reflected in the poor condition of urban streets. The study recommends that congestion costs be reflected through a system of restricted licenses (amounting to between five and seven cents a vehicle kilometer) on all use of urban streets. Several alternative schemes are outlined.

In its most general form the recommendation of the study is that road user charges be reduced in rural areas and increased in urban areas. If carried out in the manner suggested, the net impact of these changes would be to raise public revenues from user taxes by 32 to 50 percent, depending on the country. Guidelines are given on the form these taxes could take. Gasoline taxes should be gradually lowered and diesel taxes raised slightly. Import duties and general license fees should be abolished. Special licenses should be required for use of urban streets.

The large role given to congestion charges in total revenue in the proposed system may require some restructuring of the tax and expenditure responsibilities of the various levels of government. The study suggests that thought be given to using the congestion charges as a means of providing local governments, particularly in the main urban areas, with a more viable tax base. Care should be taken, however, to insure that transfers of revenue and responsibilities do not cause financial difficulties at the various levels of government.

Another possibility that should be considered is the earmarking of tax revenues for maintenance expenditures on rural and urban roads. This could serve to improve highway maintenance in some countries.

In Chapter VIII the timing of the implementation of the proposed changes is discussed. The suggested pattern (covering a period of five years) is meant to be an illustrative exercise. Considerable scope exists for varying the pattern, particularly in light of the experience gained as the implementation process proceeds. In general it is proposed that gasoline taxes, import duties and general license fees be lowered at the same time as urban congestion charges and diesel taxes are raised. The proposals should, however, be considered as part

3

of a package. Lowering some charges without raising the urban congestion charges would lead to fiscal difficulties.

The existence of a common market makes some coordination of the changes between countries desirable. This is not, however, absolutely necessary if the changes made are along the lines proposed above. The proposed system of user charges primarily affects domestic traffic with only a minor impact on inter-country trade. Lowering license fees and import duties on trucks will place all countries in the same favorable position with respect to the inter-country carry-ing trade as is currently the case with Honduras.

The above discussion has focused on the charges necessary to achieve a more efficient allocation of resources in the transport sector. In all of the Central American countries the revenues yielded by the proposed system are in excess of those currently collected. It might be considered desirable for fiscal reasons to impose higher charges on the transport sector. The study suggests that in this case taxes should be levied where they will cause the least distortion and where they can be considered most equitable. Higher annual license fees on luxury automobiles or possibly a general license duty on all vehicles are the preferable alternatives. Taxes could also be imposed on traffic where the de-mand for road services is found to be inelastic. This may be the case for urban traffic and some forms of passenger travel. In each case care should be taken to estimate the economic cost or incidence of the tax.

In addition to the traditional road taxes, the study has considered the costs imposed on transportation by deficiencies in the economic framework. A strong recommendation is made for the elimination of excessively costly border cross-ing procedures. Other deficiencies considered are in tire manufacturing and oil refining. In both cases care should be exercised to insure that protection provided these industries does not place excessive burdens on transportation.

As with the costs, there are also benefits to be derived which may fall out-side the traditional scope of user charges. These offer attractive taxing pos-sibilities when they can be readily identified. Road improvement usually bene-fits property owners in the vicinity of the road. There is considerable scope in Central America for collecting some of these benefits either directly through property taxes or indirectly through taxes on the commodities (coffee, for example) produced on this land.

Throughout the study recommendations are also made concerning the type of information that should be collected in order to facilitate the making of economic decisions in the transport sector. A partial list of these data include traffic counts, velocity studies, freight rates, maintenance costs for stretches of road, post investment studies, etc. Most of the information could be collected relatively cheaply and easily.

This study has probably raised more questions than it has answered. The

4

application of a rigorous analytical framework to the problem of road pricing has revealed the inadequacy of the current "state of the art." There were many questions raised, the answers to which could only be guessed at. One such question, for example, was what costs are incurred by the highway authorities when a given roadway is used by a vehicle of a specified weight. This question turns out to be of crucial importance if the prices charged to the road user are to allocate resources efficiently, yet the information required in order to answer it is grossly inadequate. If this study can stimulate the search for the answers to some of these questions, it will have served a very useful purpose.

II

THE ECONOMICS OF ROAD PRICING

It is imperative that the economics of road pricing be firmly established. By the economics of pricing is meant simply the impact of price upon the distribution of resources. Focusing upon the allocation of resources provides a common ground upon which rational economic decisions can be made.

Road Characteristics

Why should the pricing of road services create such difficulties? Economic theory provides many insights into how the pricing mechanism works and how it distributes resources under a variety of circumstances. The market determines the price of wheat or steel (under given circumstances or within accepted constraints), yet a great deal of uncertainty surrounds the pricing of road services. The reasons for this uncertainty must lie in the fact that roads are different from either wheat or steel. Once these differences are clearly understood, the main body of price theory provides adequate tools for the analysis of road pricing.

The inherent characteristics of road services distinguishing them from other commodities or services are: (i) the specificity of location, (ii) the joint product nature of capacity and quality, (iii) the significant economies of scale in production, and (iv) the sale of services (under state monopoly conditions). Of these four characteristics the first two are of greatest relevance to the pricing of road services.

6

Specificity of location

This is perhaps the most obvious characteristic of road services. Once a road has been built it can have no other function but to provide services along its route; that is, it is location specific. In the case of much of the output of an economy (such as wheat or steel) the plant may be fixed but the product can be transported. For highways both the plant and the services provided are paradoxically immobile. Road services between Guatemala City and San Salvador cannot be substituted for road services between San Salvador and Tegucigalpa, but wheat produced in Guatemala can be substituted for wheat produced in Honduras.

In addition to being specific in location, roads also provide specific services at a moment of time. Unlike wheat, road services cannot be stored; unused road services between 5 a.m. and 6 a.m. cannot be used between 7 a.m. and 8 a.m.

The specificity of road services with respect to spatial and temporal location means that the unused capacity of roads has in the short-run no alternative use, that is, its shadow price is zero. An unused or under-utilized road at a specific time cannot be sold at another location or time where or when there is a demand for capacity. The implications of this for the pricing of roads is that if excess capacity exists it has an economic value of zero and therefore there should be a zero price for the rent of this capacity.[1] On the other hand if the demand exceeds the capacity at zero price[2] at a given time and location there should be a rationing or congestion price, because only then does the road have an economic alternative to a use by one user—namely, use by another user.

Capacity[3] and quality: a joint product

One of the features common to many types of non-urban roads is the under-utilization of capacity.[4] If this is the case the interesting question to ask is

---

[1] This zero price refers to the price for renting the capacity. It does not mean that the price for using the road should be zero; there are real resources (the variable maintenance costs) used in the sense of a deterioration of the capacity every time a vehicle journey is made.

[2] The reverse relationship is the usual definition of a free good—excess supply at a zero price.

[3] Capacity is at best an imprecise concept. The common engineering definition of capacity appears to have little economic rationale. Capacity should be thought of as a continuum—a road can handle a varying volume of traffic, but each volume is carried at a different cost. Throughout this study capacity is used in this sense.

[4] This may not be true for all non-urban roads, but is a generalization that appears applicable to a major part of the non-urban network of most countries. In any case it is open to empirical verification.

why does this excess capacity exist. The answer would appear to lie in two characteristics of roads: capacity is a joint product of quality, and there are substantial discontinuities in the construction of roads.[5]

A common reason for investing in road improvements is the fact that improvements lower the transport costs of existing traffic. The IBRD in its appraisal of a project to pave the Western Highway in Honduras said, "The savings in vehicle operating costs will produce rates of return ranging from 11 percent to 25 percent for individual sections, all of which are adequate to justify the proposed investment."[6] This improvement is to be made on a good gravel road of 246 km with an average daily traffic count of between 100 and 250 vehicles (1966) per day. Although this is by any standard an uncongested road, it still pays to pave the road and thereby further increase capacity.[7] Thus it appears that increased capacity is a by-product when the quality of roads is improved; or more accurately, quality and capacity are joint products.

The implications of the joint product nature of road investment are important for the pricing of road services. If quality and capacity are indeed joint products (and the Central American experience supports this argument) then it is likely that many roads will have excess capacity even when optimally developed, and that in order to optimize the use of resources, the pricing of road services must take into account the existence of this excess capacity. If unused capacity exists it clearly has no alternative use and therefore becomes a free good similar to air. If on the other hand the demand exceeds the capacity, a positive price serves as a device for allocating the scarce roads between competitive uses.

Discontinuities in investment

Given the joint product nature of capacity and quality, the problem of discontinuities in road investment no longer becomes of crucial importance in rationalizing the existence of excess capacity in road services. If, however, these discontinuities or "lumpiness" do exist, it adds to the argument that many roads will have excess capacity (or conversely congestion) at a given point in time. It means that only rarely will it be possible to supply road services in quantities such that supply satisfies demand at a price that just covers average costs.

---

[5] A more trivial answer would be that road planners make mistakes, but the generality of this observed excess capacity suggests that the answer is elsewhere.

[6] IBRD Report No. TO–584a. "Appraisal of the Western Highway Paving Project, Honduras." 1967.

[7] Congestion and its definitions are discussed in Chapter VII.

Roads as a natural monopoly

The provision of road services is usually under conditions of monopoly. The degree of monopoly power will, however, vary according to the availability of alternative modes of transport such as railways, waterways, or alternative roads. Road services are similar to many other public utilities with respect to the problems of the pricing of its services. These public utilities are generally regulated with the intention of preventing them from fully exploiting their monopoly power. Regulations often take the form of limiting rates of return or, more crudely stated, of preventing the monopoly from making too much money. The basis of this form of regulation is on grounds of equity, that is, it is "fair" or "right." The economic basis for regulating such monopolies is that they restrict output by fixing prices above marginal costs in order to maximize profits. Regulations that fix rates of return but that do not specify prices do not necessarily optimize the distribution of resources. They may in fact lead to serious distortions depending upon the actual pricing policy followed. These distortions may lead to serious misallocation of resources in cases where output and capacity are closely related, as in an electric power network. They may also be extremely important where either excess or under-capacity is a common occurrence, such as in roads. Road services should be priced so as not to wastefully restrict their use in the case of under-utilized capacity, and so as to ration the road space between potential users in the case of deficient or restricted capacity.

The government may, however, wish to exploit its monopoly position in order to foster other goals such as increasing public revenues or redistributing income. In this case modifications in the pricing rules will be necessary. The form of these modifications is extremely important as different forms will lead to different patterns of resource allocation.

The Pricing of Road Services

The price for using a road should be equal to the value of the resource consumed due to the use of the road. Every time a vehicle makes a trip down a road it does a certain amount of damage to the road surface. Where there is congestion additional costs will be borne by other users of the road. These are the real economic costs of using the services of a road. (The private vehicle running costs are not considered here as these are generally priced in a reasonably competitive market and thus would have only a minor and indirect influence on solutions to the problem of pricing the road services provided by the public authorities.) These costs are equal to the variable maintenance costs[8]

---

[8] Defined as the additional costs generated by one more vehicle (or decision-making unit) using the road.

9

plus the costs of congestion. The price charged to cover these costs, the economic user charge (EUC), is the price to be charged in order to optimize the allocation of resources.[9]

This conclusion is neither surprising nor startling; it is the usual pricing prescription of economic theory that price equal marginal cost. The difficulties in accepting this pricing prescription arise out of the fact that it is not possible to say a priori whether the road budget will be in deficit or in surplus. In particular if a large part of the road network has excess capacity, a deficit will occur which implies that financial transfers must take place. It is possible, however, that congestion costs on the rest of the network are such that the charges required to cover these would more than offset this deficit. This is a question of empirical verification. In any case it is important to distinguish the two separate arguments; one says that the resources are best allocated by pricing services at marginal costs, the other is an argument about the financing of roads and therefore about the distribution of the benefits from the roads.

This distinction is crucial because it can be a major source of confusion. By using the EUC the maximum net benefits are obtained from the road network. If the resulting distribution of benefits is unacceptable, it does not mean that the EUC should be rejected, but rather that the focus should be on how to redistribute the greater amount of net benefits obtained by using the EUC. Any attempt to redistribute these benefits by prices for road services greater or less than the EUC will result in a smaller bundle of net benefits.

The most efficient use of the road network is obtained by prices equal to marginal costs, but how is the most equitable distribution of benefits obtained? For this there can be no simple answer; decisions about equity involve value judgments. Several criteria can be used to levy road user taxes[10] (ability to pay, benefits received, ease of collection, etc.). The important fact is that it is income that is being redistributed not transport being made more efficient. This implies a different set of taxes and not necessarily ones associated directly with the use of roads.

The connection between those taxes levied to achieve income redistribution and the use of the roads becomes even more remote when the benefit principle is used. There is often no connection between the use of a road and the benefits received. A large part of the demand for transport services is generally a derived demand, transport being an intermediate good or service. As such the benefits of lower transport costs occur not to the sellers of transport services

---

[9] Difficulties associated with non-competitive conditions in the rest of the economy and fiscal exigencies are discussed below.

[10] By road user taxes are meant those charges not related to the costs of using the road and not necessary to achieve economic efficiency.

but to the producers and consumers of the goods transported.[11] If in the example used above the poor consume the products transported, attempts to redistribute income by levying charges above the EUC on the use of the roads will have a regressive income effect. One such benefit tax that has the appeal of retaining efficiency in resource distribution is the land tax. When a road is built or improved, the benefits often accrue to the inelastic factor of production, land, and are visible in the form of increased rents. Thus an income redistribution, which many would consider just and desirable, could be achieved by means of taxes on the incremental rents.[12] This tax is not necessary to achieve the efficient use of the road network; the EUC is sufficient and necessary for this.

Non-competitive pricing

The basic assumption behind the marginal cost pricing for road services is that competitive conditions exist elsewhere in the economy; all goods are sold at marginal cost and all factors receive their marginal product. This is, however, an idealization of the real world where, because of taxes, externalities and monopoly, some degree of non-competitive pricing (prices above or below marginal costs) exists. This suggests the possibility of second best solutions where transport prices differ from marginal costs so as to compensate for deviations from marginal cost pricing in other sectors of the economy.[13]

Such solutions involve formidable practical difficulties due to the large amount of information required. The cost of gathering this information is likely to be prohibitive and it is not possible to formulate simple rules for handling such situations. Each case will be difficult and different.

There still remains the necessity of making policy decisions about second best pricing. The basis must be marginal costs (including rents resulting from congestion), for these will reflect the real or alternative costs of using resources in a generally competitive environment. It may be necessary, however, to deviate from marginal cost prices (the EUC) where sufficiently severe non-competitive conditions exist in some sectors of the economy.

Fortunately for the decision-maker, the complexities introduced by attempting second best solutions are likely to yield small returns in most cases. Most economies, particularly those of the underdeveloped world, have a fairly strong competitive character, usually dominated by an agricultural or extractive sector

---

[11] Except in the case where transport services are sold under non-competitive conditions.

[12] Or more precisely on the consumer surpluses generated by the road investment.

[13] See R. G. Lipsey and Kelvin Lancaster, "The General Theory of Second Best," *Review of Economics and Statistics*, XXIV (1955–56), pp. 11–32.

with the non-competitive sectors operating at the fringes. In addition, the derived demand for transport services on the part of these fringe industries is likely to be inelastic,[14] in part because transport costs and a fortiori user charges are a minor part of their total costs. The leverage to be obtained in order to change output by manipulating user charges is thus small even for transport taxes that are fairly large relative to transport costs. In any case the correction of distortions introduced by non-competitive pricing is usually better handled directly through prevention of the conditions which allow monopoly to exist rather than through the manipulation of transport prices. Public policy has at its disposal means other than transport rates or road user charges which can be used in its efforts to control non-competitive behavior.

Intermodal competition

The complexities that arise due to the existence of competing modes of transport, usually road and rail, raise the question of whether marginal cost pricing is the appropriate policy to be followed in the case of the highway. The usual argument is that since railroads must meet overhead or capital costs roads should do the same, equality of constraints being somehow regarded as "fair." This, however, does not focus on the economics of pricing but once again confuses the issue by mixing both efficiency and equity considerations.

If railroad pricing is subject to the same economic analysis as road pricing the answer is the same: prices should be equal to marginal costs. If roads are also priced at marginal cost (EUC), the prices facing the user of transport services reflect the real economic cost to the economy providing these services. Thus if the user chooses to transport by rail (because it is cheaper) he will be minimizing his costs and at the same time maximizing the benefits to the economy from its transportation services. If prices reflect real or alternative costs, no problems of transport coordination or tax "neutrality" are encountered, and the mechanism of the market place is sufficient to insure that maximum benefits are achieved.

Marginal cost pricing on the railroads does not mean that the railroads will necessarily operate with a financial deficit as is the case with non-congested highways. With no excess rail capacity, marginal cost pricing may be sufficient to cover all financial costs; on the other hand, if excess capacity exists, a deficit will occur.

Most of the world's railroads do operate with a chronic financial deficit. This is the result mainly of excess capacity which exists for historical reasons. The size of the railroads combined with public ownership or regulation has

---

[14] Non-competitive behavior is common to those industries with complex production functions or high capital requirements where the value added by transport is likely to be small.

made it difficult to revalue the capital stock of the railroads down to a level reflecting current conditions or to change the services provided. Railroads are thus often saddled with book costs which do not reflect present value, and in addition, they have frequently been used as a social welfare institution by providing services to certain classes of users at less than marginal costs (e.g., much of the passenger traffic of many railroads) and by subsidizing certain classes of labor (e.g., the Guatemalan railroad). The large railroad deficits have little to do with the efficient allocation of transportation resources. They are more properly related to considerations of equity rather than of economic efficiency.

The departure from marginal cost pricing by the railroads has two effects: a loss in net benefits caused by a decrease in total transport services produced, and a reduction in net benefits caused by the transfer of some traffic to less efficient highway transport. These losses are kept to a minimum if the railroads meet the financial constraints (such as earning a rate of return on book value of capital assets) by levying charges above marginal costs on those services where demand elasticity is lowest, since the elasticity of demand for rail services reflects both the absolute loss in total traffic and the transfer to roads.

The departure of the railroads from marginal cost pricing suggests that deviations from marginal conditions in railroads should be matched by similar deviations from marginal conditions for competing services. If, for example, some railroad services are priced above marginal costs with the result that traffic is shifted to roads at a higher economic cost than if it had moved by rail, the possibility arises of shifting this traffic back to rails by means of a road tax.[15] This tax would restore the distribution of traffic between road and rail, but it would result in an additional loss in total traffic. This lost traffic, which if carried would yield benefits in excess of the value of resources used up, would as a result of the "equalizing" tax promise benefits to the shipper less than the cost (including the tax) and thus the traffic would not move. With this type of tax the net benefits achieved by moving some traffic more efficiently (e.g., by rail rather than road) must be weighted against the net loss from the failure of lost traffic to move at all. No a priori statement can be made to support the contention that the result of adding these "neutralizing" taxes is to increase welfare, except on the assumption that the demand for transportation affected by the "equalizing tax" has negligible elasticity.

As a practical fact the placement of "neutralizing" taxes on road services will be a dubious process. The generally competitive nature of the highway transport industry will not permit the impact of this tax to be selective. A levy such as licenses on trucks will raise average costs and be reflected under com-

---

[15] A tax above the *EUC*.

13

petitive conditions in increased prices for all truck transport services—not just those affected by rail competition. The same difficulty arises with general tire or gas taxes, import duties, etc. The likely result is that any simple tax, rather than neutralizing the traffic structure distortions introduced by the constraints imposed on rails, will produce a structure in which most road services are overpriced. In order to avoid this taxes would have to be placed on narrowly defined services, that is, on particular commodities and particular routes. This would require a great deal of information and an administrative system of great complexity.[16]

The upshot of these considerations is that it is in general advisable to tolerate a certain amount of misallocation of traffic between road and rail rather than to attempt to eliminate this misallocation completely by road taxes. This would almost inevitably result in some traffic that could move economically by road not moving at all. The existence of rail rates above marginal cost on traffic that is competitive with road is a justification for raising road costs by charges somewhat above what would be justifiable on other grounds—but only in general a small fraction of the distance needed to equalize the differentials between road and rail with the differentials in marginal cost. This fraction would be derived from a comparison of the importance and cross-elasticity of traffic for which the choice is primarily between road and rail and the elasticity and importance of traffic for which the choice is primarily between road haulage and not moving at all. This is admittedly a somewhat difficult principle to apply in practice, given the uncertainties involved in these various elasticities, but given the constraints placed on the railroad, it probably comes as close to an optimal solution as is possible. Even so, the net gain from such a policy as compared with one of making no attempt at all to levy offsetting road taxes may be so slight as hardly to warrant the complexities involved. In any case this problem would be alleviated if the cost of achieving the distributional and social objectives sought by setting railroad rates below cost were met by subventions out of general revenues. Otherwise these costs must be met by cross-subsidization by raising other rail rates, and thus exacerbating the misallocation between road and rail.

The Long Run: Location and Investment

Under normal circumstances price usually performs two functions: first it adjusts demand to existing supply, and secondly it gives signals as to whether

---

[16] It would be necessary to know the distortions caused by the rail pricing policy, the elasticity of demand for transport for all commodities, the cross-elasticity of demand between transport modes and the impact of all taxes on the distribution resources.

production should be expanded or contracted. In cases where goods or services are sold under competitive conditions and where there are no externalities, the rationing price provides useful signals for the investment decision. Where these conditions are not met, as in the case of road services, the signals given by price are of limited usefulness for roadway investment decisions. Price in this case is primarily a short-run phenomenon whose function is to ration existing supply with existing demand. It is nevertheless useful to examine the effect of this price upon the distribution of resources over time. There are two areas in which the price of road services are of relevance to the investment decision: public investment decisions with respect to the investment in roads, and private investment decisions with respect to the location of economic activity. Each of these will be discussed in turn.

Public investment in highways

The pricing of road services is in principle prior to the decision to expand or improve the highway network. Investment decisions should be based upon the expected benefits over and above estimated costs. Whether or not the public authorities recapture some of these benefits through special taxation should be held irrelevant in decisions concerning investment and the efficient use of the highway.[17] If the public authorities do not collect the benefits they will accrue to someone else in the economy; if this distribution of the benefits is considered inequitable the problem then becomes one of redistribution.

It is important for maximizing benefits that the correct pricing policy—that of charging the EUC—be followed. If a price above the EUC is charged and there is some elasticity in the demand for road services, the benefits will be less than those available if the EUC were levied. This may in some cases lead to a rejection of a potentially worthwhile project because the full benefits from generated traffic will not be realized. Conversely, charging a price below the EUC can lead to excessive investment which seemingly is justified by the number of vehicles using or expected to use the new or improved road.[18] Given a pricing policy it is possible to calculate a conditional optimum investment policy. But clearly since the actual investment decision depends on the pricing policy, the overall best investment decision will be made only in association with the optimum pricing policy. If for fiscal or other reasons the optimal pricing policy is not expected to be followed, the second best investment decision under these constraints may call for either more or less investment than the optimal level appropriate to optimal pricing.

---

[17] The term taxation is more appropriate than that of road user charges, for the relationship between benefits and the use of the road may be quite obscure.

[18] This does not, however, appear to be the case in Central America. See Chapter VII.

15

One of the alleged disadvantages of short-run marginal cost pricing (EUC) is that it provides no signal for the investment decision. It is unfortunately true that the signals provided are less direct than are provided in competitive industry, but this difficulty is inherent in any system of road management. If, for example, sufficient taxes were levied on road users to cover the annual capital and maintenance costs of a road, this does not then demonstrate conclusively that there were enough benefits to have justified the expenditure. It does show this, in general, for an isolated road. However, if a new improved road is built parallel to an old one, it may attract enough traffic so that the taxes paid by the traffic using it will pay for it even though the gain in cost over the use of the old road is only a fraction of the cost of the new. It does not say much about future investments in roads in other places; each of these roads will require that benefits and costs be calculated. The fact that one road could be made to pay for itself may provide an interesting check on the cost-benefit calculations or methodology, but this information has been obtained at the expense of some benefits foregone (obtainable at zero economic cost) through loss of traffic which would have used the road at a price sufficient to cover the damage done, that is, the EUC. The signal obtained may also be quite misleading as to whether or not a project was justified. If revenues are insufficient to cover annual capital and maintenance costs it cannot be said that this was not an economic project because only part of the benefits are represented by the price. The information obtained (at some cost) through this type of pricing can at best only be remotely connected with the investment decision. No signal is given as to whether a road should be expanded or contracted. Thus there appears to be no real alternative to estimating benefits and costs in making the investment decision. Correct pricing (the EUC) is necessary but is not of much help. On the other hand, incorrect pricing (some version of full costs) is not of much help either and may, in fact, be very misleading.

Location of economic activity

It is important to trace the effect of user charges upon the location of economic activity. It is sometimes argued that pricing below full costs (however defined) will cause firms to locate inefficiently. This is incorrect. Consider the case of the government which after making the appropriate cost-benefit calculation, builds a road from points A to B. The location decision of firms will be based upon their estimate of the benefits to be gained from locating in one place rather than another. This should be part of the same estimate of benefits made by the government when the decision was made to build the road. The individual firm will be faced with two variables in making its decision, the cost of transport and the other advantages. If the EUC is levied the real resource cost of using the road will be automatically included in the location decision. The question is: Will the mechanism of the market then handle the problem of where to locate? The answer is yes; each location will have a rent associated with it which will appear to the firm as the cost differential of various locations. The usual form of such rents will be the increased land rents resulting from the construction of the road. This is, of course, one form in which the estimates of the benefits used in making the decision to build the road appear ex post. It makes no difference whether or not the government by taxation appropriates these benefits or rents because, regardless of government tax policy, these rents will enter into the location decision as a cost. In one case the rents accrue to the holders of the land and in the other case to the government. Either way they serve to ration the land to its most productive uses.

One problem that does arise with respect to the government investment decision and the location of economic activity is the lead-lag question; that is, does the government build the road and then the location of economic activity take place, or vice versa? If the government takes the lead using the surplus or cost-benefit criterion to make its decision, no problems are encountered. If, on the other hand, the government is in a position of reacting to decisions already made it is conceivable that a misallocation of resources could take place. Suppose, for example, the best economic location of a fairly large firm is in Tegucigalpa where the market is, but for some reason it decides to locate in Jutigalpa. After the firm has located in Jutigalpa the government then adds up the costs and benefits and decides to pave the road between Tegucigalpa and Jutigalpa. Before the firm located in Jutigalpa this was an uneconomic project, but after the location decision it becomes justified; thus it would appear as though the government could be led by firms in making its investment decisions. Indeed, if in locating in Jutigalpa the firm could anticipate that this would lead the government to pave the road (and not require the firm to pay special taxes to cover the cost) the firm might well be induced to make the postulated wrong decision.

There appears to be no simple solution to this case; perhaps a combination of once and for all location taxes combined with the government refusing to bail out firms on occasion (i.e., to increase the risk to the firm) would be sufficient to discourage firms from making the wrong location decision.[19] It is unlikely that any one firm would be willing to add to the existing risks of

---

[19] See Walters, Chapter IV for a more detailed discussion of this problem and the type of solutions that may be employed. The most likely case of firms leading government is in suburban development where developers operate on a sufficient scale so as to insure government actions. This does not necessarily lead to bad investment decisions.

making a location decision the risks involved in securing favorable government action.

Non-Road Taxes

The above sections have discussed the traditional or common types of road taxes with reference to the costs of using roads and their effect on government revenues. In addition to these traditional types of taxes there are other taxes only indirectly connected with the use of the road which offer possibilities for raising public revenues. These are the taxes which attempt to capture for the public sector some of the benefits that arise from road investment. When the decision is made to make an investment in roads, it is done presumably by estimating the net benefits, which then appear as increases in income or wealth to some sectors of the economy. These increases in benefits can then be considered within the legitimate scope of tax policy. The taxing away of these benefits is not necessary, however, to achieve the efficient allocation of resources within the economy. Only the EUC and a rational road investment policy are necessary for this.

Taxing the benefits that arise from public expenditures has intuitive appeal; it fits nicely with the tax criteria that those who benefit should pay and also that payment should be in accordance with ability to pay. In addition it conforms to commonly accepted financial criteria; if the investment were justified there should be sufficient benefits available to cover all costs including the capital or financial charges. Thus the solution to problems of highway financing appears to be in the form of a type of two-part tariff, one part of which (the EUC) covers the cost of using the road, and one part (the benefit taxes) covering the capital costs or financial transfers. This type of taxation is in principle unobjectionable, but as a practical policy suffers from some limitations—chiefly the difficulty of devising taxes that will adequately approximate the increase in benefits without impact at the margin on use of the facility.

The benefits may not be directly connected with the use of the road,[20] and thus this type of tax policy may lead to a movement away from the traditional road taxes, possibly in the direction of property and commodity taxes. Suppose the government decides, after adding up the costs and benefits, to build a road from a forest area to the sea, and upon completion of the road a lumbering

---

[20] It should be obvious that the benefits, at least in some cases, are unlikely to accrue to the physical users of the roads. Take, for example, a competitive trucking industry (as is found in Central America); its rate of return should be the same after the improvement (allowing for some minor lags) as before the improvement. The industry does not receive the benefits, although this is quite commonly believed to be the case.

18

operation starts. If the lumber industry sells in a competitive market and if this operation is too small to significantly affect the market price, the benefits of the road will accrue to the owners of the timber lands with access to the road (at least if there is adequate competition among lumbering and sawmill operators). They receive the benefits of the public expenditure and thus become liable for the benefit tax. The exact form of the tax could vary considerably. It could be in the form of a concession charge, an annual license fee, a stumpage charge, a property tax, etc. Here it was relatively simple to identify the beneficiaries; in most situations this is not likely to be the case. Take, for example, the case of a highway connecting two urban centers. An improvement in the highway results in the lowering of transport costs of all goods and passengers carried between the two cities. How are the benefits distributed? If the commodities number in the thousands it is probably impossible to say, as the increase in benefits would depend on the derived demand for transport for each commodity and the market conditions under which the commodities are produced and distributed. If the commodity is produced and distributed under competitive conditions the benefits will be divided between producers (the factors of production) and consumers of the product, depending on their various supply and demand elasticities. On the other hand, if the product is distributed under monopoly conditions the benefits of lower transport costs may be captured by the monopoly. A whole range of possibilities exists and it would be extremely difficult to trace the benefits to taxable units.

In those circumstances where there is a wide but unidentifiable distribution of the benefits it may be better to forgo an attempt to collect them and instead rely on more general tax measures such as income taxes. This assumes that the benefits are distributed sufficiently widely so that redistribution through the tax system for purposes of equity is unnecessary. A practical policy might be one in which benefits are taxed whenever readily identifiable (such as in the case of the lumbering operation above), and when they are not so readily identifiable (or taxable) more general tax measures would be used to finance highways. In any case the best policy does not necessarily involve taxes other than the traditional road taxes if efficient road use is to be achieved.

Two points should emerge from this discussion: one, that benefits do not occur in proportion to use of highway facilities, nor do they necessarily occur to the immediate user of the facilities;[21] and two, that taxation of the benefits is unnecessary to achieve the efficient allocation of resources but may be a useful and equitable way of collecting taxes and of financing road expenditure.

---

[21] An exception would be the case of a monopolized, or rigidly regulated, transport industry where all benefits could accrue to the transport firm itself.

19

Pricing Policy

The principal focus of pricing policy is to charge the EUC. This does not mean, however, that the pricing policy of every country should be to charge only the EUC. This may be indeed the prescription of the theoretical analysis, but the analysis is only as good as the assumptions upon which it is based and the prescription must be relevant to the goals desired. If, for example, non-competitive sectors exist in the economy, it is desirable (although difficult) to take this fact into account in deriving a pricing policy which will deviate somewhat from charging the EUC. Also, if goals are changed from optimizing benefits in general to optimizing them for a specific group the pricing rules can be appropriately adjusted. Other goals such as balancing the road budget or raising a specific sum of taxes from road transport can also be used as constraints to which the modification of the change away from the EUC must conform. The framework permits the analysis of the consequences, in terms of resource allocation, of each or all of these policy aims. Each aim will have its costs and its benefits as well as a different set of road taxes and prices. These costs can, however, be analyzed only in terms of their impact on resource allocation; this would in turn require a theory with some clear optimizing properties.

If the analysis is correct, it is difficult to fault the conclusion that, given the assumptions regarding competition, charging the EUC is the best pricing policy. Other aims and assumptions imply a modification of this price; they do not imply abandoning the EUC standard altogether in favor of other "theories" of road pricing.

Nevertheless, the popularity of some of these "policies" or "theories" makes a brief examination of them worthwhile; at the same time it will also serve to point out their inappropriateness when compared to the framework that has been discussed.[22] The most common of these theories is what might be called the average cost doctrine. This doctrine says that the costs of the road should be paid by the vehicles using the road.[23] This doctrine appears to have no maximizing properties with respect to the allocation of resources. Furthermore it is difficult to define costs (Which are they—historical costs, replacement costs, market value?) and to determine the distribution of these costs between users, over the vehicle population and over time. At best a number of arbitrary decisions must be made regarding their allocation. It is not possible to determine these cost allocations within the context of resource optimization. In contrast, the framework used in this study is quite unequivocal about what are

---

[22] This will be made more obvious in the discussion of individual taxes that follows in Chapter V.

[23] See Walters, Chapter IV, for a more detailed discussion.

real costs and how they should be distributed.[24] In addition the average cost doctrine says nothing about what taxes should be levied (all taxes are equivalent, only the total matters) while the framework used in this study is quite specific (see Chapter V) about the type of taxes and their impact on the allocation of resources.

Similar difficulties are encountered with what might be termed the long-run marginal cost doctrine. It is not possible to define the concept in an economically meaningful way. Again arbitrary decisions must be made with respect to future traffic flows and the allocation of costs over the vehicle population and over time. Also, no clear maximizing properties are present. It is always possible to show that a better utilization of resources could be achieved by deviating from the defined long-run, marginal cost price. The difficulties of this and other such theories becomes obvious when they are attempted in practice, for they can be implemented only by making a series of arbitrary decisions with no relevance to optimum resource allocation. There is also no way of relating these pricing prescriptions to either policy aims or the assumptions made about the economy.[25]

The goals of road pricing policy

The goals of public policy are not always readily discernible. More often than not this lack of any specified goal is the result of a combination of conflicting policies. Thus a government's policy may be to promote rapid economic growth by the best utilization of its transport system, but at the same time it may wish to promote the welfare of groups such as railroad labor. The aims of policy with respect to road pricing (or pricing of transport services in general) can be considered as falling into three rough categories: one, utilizing resources including transport capital as efficiently as possible; two, redistributing income; and three, as a source of public revenues. These policies need not conflict, but it is likely that one goal can be pushed only at the expense of the others.

There is little dispute about the first of these being a desirable goal; the dispute is usually as to how this is to be achieved. This goal has been the principal focus of the framework outlined in this chapter and reflects the preoccupation of the economist with the optimum utilization of resources.

This is, of course, not the only goal of policy; some growth can be sacrificed in order to obtain what the society considers a better distribution of income.

---

[24] It is not clear whether this applies to individual roads or to the road system as a whole.

[25] In the case of non-competitive sectors in the economy where a second best solution is implied, average cost or long-run marginal cost pricing have no guides to offer the policy-maker.

This is not easy to achieve through road pricing. The incidence of most road taxes is so indirect as to make it difficult or almost impossible to achieve significant effects on the equality or inequality of income by shifts among these taxes. It is possible, however, to have a system of charges and taxes that affects some groups more than others. Taxes can be designed so as to favor the railroad and thus the specialized factors of production used by the railroad. Any number of similar discriminations are possible, but there is a constant danger that they will be used to protect vested interests rather than to implement a conscious and systematic set of pricing policies or to equalize income distribution.

The third goal, that of raising revenues, is largely a matter of alternative means of taxation. Certain forms of road taxes present more attractive forms of taxation. Some are more easily collected or are more politically acceptable, etc. Care must be taken, however, to insure that these taxes are not more likely to cause distortions than the alternatives available. Transportation is in large measure an intermediate good or service, and taxation of it can have repercussions on production efficiency in a wide range of outputs.

The above goals are not meant to be exhaustive; they merely try to point out common features found in most public transport pricing policies. It is always possible to disagree with the particular combination of policies followed, but it is nevertheless possible to make meaningful economic statements within the constraints imposed by these policies. The framework developed in this chapter has this flexibility. While the goal of an efficient use of resources is stressed, this still can encompass a variety of aims. If, for example, road taxes are desired for public revenues, there are some taxes that are better than others —the best ones being those that minimize the impact on the allocation of resources. The stress is thus on the economics of road pricing.

III

THE TRANSPORTATION SYSTEM
IN CENTRAL AMERICA

Transportation and the Economy: An Overview

The main focus of this study is the pricing of road services. This cannot be done in a vacuum, however; policy must be formulated within the constraints imposed by the real world. This chapter will attempt to provide the context within which the policy decisions must be made. It is intended to be more in the nature of a general summary or an overview of the economy and its transportation network rather than a comprehensive survey. The more comprehensive surveys have already been done.[1]

The Central American economy

In the past the Central American countries have developed along strictly national lines, with each country having closer links through trade to the external world than to each other. The result of this is a transportation system with an orientation towards external or international trade. The major transportation routes tend to be between each region's major producing and consuming areas and the sea. This outward looking orientation is, however, gradually changing.

---

[1] See IBRD Report No. WH–170a, *Economic Development and Prospects of Central America*, June 5, 1967, and T.S.C. Consortium, *Central American Transport Study*, 1964–65.

The development of the Pan American Highway in the late 1930's and the impetus it received during World War II contributed greatly to the breakdown of the geographically imposed isolationism. In recent years this breakdown has been accelerated by the moves toward a common regional market.

The five countries that make up the common market have an area of 171 thousand square miles and a population of 15.5 million (1969). A great deal of diversity not revealed in the aggregate data is to be found among these countries. El Salvador has a population density of 255 persons per square kilometer, while Honduras has only 36 persons per square kilometer. The rate of growth of population in Guatemala is three percent per annum while that of Costa Rica is 3.7 percent. Per capita incomes range from US$260 in Honduras to US$510 in Costa Rica. There are, however, many features in common: in all the countries exports of primary commodities (mainly coffee, bananas and cotton) are the principal determinants of the rate of growth; the economies are primarily rural and agricultural but with rapidly growing urban centers; and the general administrative and organizational structure of the economies bear a close resemblance to one another.

The last two decades have seen substantial changes in these countries as more and more development has taken place outside the traditional sectors. A modern infrastructure of power, communications and transport is evolving and, under the stimulus of protected markets, some light industry. In recent years the goal of a common market has become a preoccupation of policymakers and moves in this direction have been made through the formation of a customs union. This has stimulated trade between the countries, chiefly in the form of goods previously imported from outside Central America. This trade is gradually taking on a wider aspect with more commodities being traded as new transportation links are established and old ones improved.

The development of the Central American region has taken place within the framework of a market economy. The importance of the export sector which has had to compete on an international level has helped reinforce this direction. Traditionally government has been restricted to providing largely administrative services, but with the increasing emphasis upon economic development the government has expanded its role. This role, as is to be expected given the agricultural nature of the economy, still remains relatively small with government expenditures around 10 percent of national income. Given this laissez-faire atmosphere, government attempts at regulation of the economy (as, for example, limiting weights of vehicles on the highways) have not been too successful. Many regulations exist on paper but are often not carried through with much enthusiasm.

Government policy has had some impact in the establishment of protected industries. The common market movement occurred at the same time import substitution was rising in popularity, and the formulation of a customs union provided the opportunity to raise tariff levels. Tariffs have become protective in aim rather than revenue raising. This has stimulated some light industry and increased interregional trade of its products. Attempts have been made to limit regional competition in some industries (tires) but the lack of agreement as to which country should have the industry has meant limited success. The more usual pattern is a proliferation of each type of industry in each country. This has been costly in cases where economies of scale exist, (as in petroleum refining) but less costly in those such as the shirt and shoe industries. In recent years the government has become more aware of some of the adverse effects of protection.

The recent development of an effective form of interregional integration has placed the modern highway in a key position in the transportation network. Distances between regions are short, and this combined with the historically increasing efficiency of truck transport has given highways a strong comparative advantage over other forms of transport—particularly rail. In the past rail transport played an important role in moving exports and imports but their role in the future transport network is increasingly in doubt.[2] All railroads are of narrow gauge, operating for the most part with obsolete equipment and with the exception of the San Jose-Limon link in Costa Rica[3] paralleled by highways. All signs point to the increasing dominance of road transport both in interregional and external trade.

The highway network and road transport

From the map on page 60 the development pattern of the highway network is obvious; highways have developed along the agricultural regions of the Pacific plain and the central highlands. The more inhospitable regions of the Atlantic plain are virtually undeveloped; only in Guatemala is there a paved road linking the central highland to the eastern seaboard. The improvement and paving of the western (CA4) and northern (CA5) highways in Honduras provided two additional east-west links. These two links combined with the construction of the rest of the interregional network (see map)—most of which is already underway or in the planning stages—will give the region its main overland links.

In general highway construction has been rapid, averaging increases in length of about 11 percent per year (1953–65) for all-weather roads. Most of the increases took place in El Salvador, Nicaragua and Costa Rica, with Guatemala and Honduras lagging behind with rates of increase of six and five

---

[2] See IBRD Report No. WH–170a, Transport Annex.

[3] This highway link has high priority in the investment program of Costa Rica.

25

percent respectively. Both these countries have large underdeveloped areas with difficult terrain for highway construction. In addition, Honduras is the most underdeveloped of the common market members; the same might be said for large parts of Guatemala, which remain virtually outside the workings of the market economy. Honduras, however, has launched an ambitious highway program with the assistance of external aid and within a few years should have an adequate primary road network.

Nearly all of the investment in highways has taken place outside the urban areas, thus creating a gap in the overall highway network. Urban areas are very congested (see Chapter VII) but still account for up to one-fourth of all vehicle kilometers travelled. No serious plans are underway for improving this situation and nothing is likely to happen until major improvements are made in municipal administration and financing.

Use of the highway network. Over fifty percent of all cocoa, sugar, corn, beans, rice, plaintains, sesame, dairy products, tobacco, meat, forest products, minerals, etc. of the region are moved by highway transport. For the major export commodities—coffee, bananas and cotton—the railroads play a more important but a gradually diminishing role. Most of the traffic is on the paved roads of the primary highway network (Table 3.1).

TABLE 3.1: **Daily and Annual Vehicle Kilometers, Rural and Urban Roads in Central America, 1966**

	Guatemala	Honduras	El Salvador	Nicaragua	Costa Rica
Daily Vehicle Kilometers					
(*in thousands*)					
Rural					
Paved	1,490	237	1,239	976	931
Gravel	585	219	203	63	287
Dirt	38	128	173	102	120
Subtotal	2,113	584	1,615	1,141	1,338
Urban	704	300	540	381	612
Total	2,817	884	2,155	1,522	1,950
Annual Vehicle Kilometers[a]					
(*in millions*)					
Rural	770	213	586	418	488
Urban	257	110	197	140	228
Total	1,027	323	783	558	716
Average per registered vehicle (in km)	16,700	17,100	19,200	20,200	17,200

[a] Daily vehicle kilometers times 365.

Notes:

1. In Costa Rica, Nicaragua and El Salvador fairly extensive traffic counts exist in the rural areas. The difference between gravel and dirt roads is, however, poorly defined in these

Vehicle population. Data on vehicle registrations are not very reliable in most of the countries. Classification systems also differ considerably. Table 3.2 shows the composition of the current vehicle fleet on the basis of the best

---

countries. No traffic counts exist on most dirt or feeder roads. In all countries an ADT of 25 vehicles per day was assumed for this class of road.

2. In Guatemala and Honduras the traffic count data are much less extensive. For Guatemala the counts covered only part of the network. For the remainder of the network a count of 100 vehicles per day was assumed for gravel roads and 25 per day on dirt roads.

3. Only Costa Rica has urban traffic counts and these only for the central business district. A vehicle count of 1000 vehicles per day was assumed for the remainder of the urban road network in San Jose. In Guatemala, Nicaragua and El Salvador urban vehicle kilometers were assumed to be one-third of rural vehicle kilometers. In Honduras the assumption was 150 kilometers of urban streets with an ADT of 2000 per day.

4. The urban vehicle kilometer estimates were then checked for internal consistency. In Guatemala and El Salvador the assumed one-third of rural vehicle kilometers is equivalent to an ADT of 1000 per kilometer of urban street. (No data are available on the number of kilometers of urban streets in Nicaragua.)

5. Traffic count data are very poor in Honduras and the estimate of rural vehicle kilometers is an educated guess made by assuming the ADT on various classes of roads. The assumed ADT counts are probably on the high side but this was necessary to get some degree of consistency with fuel consumption and vehicle registrations. This is also the reason why an ADT of 2000 was assumed for urban streets—the one-third assumption used in the other cities would be inconsistent with vehicle registrations and fuel consumption. In addition 50 percent of all vehicles in the country are registered in the capital city.

6. The estimate of vehicle kilometers is roughly consistent with the average annual kilometers per vehicle. Observers indicated an average of 15,000 km for a passenger car was normal in most countries with a higher average for trucks. If anything this check indicates that the estimate of vehicle kilometers is on the low side in some countries—given the high percentage of trucks registered one would expect an average much higher than the 16–17,000 indicated for some countries.

7. An additional check for consistency was made with fuel consumption figures. A study in Costa Rica indicates that 76 percent of all gasoline produced (or imported) is used by motor vehicles. The figure for diesel was 26 percent. These percentages were applied to the consumption figures of the other countries:

Fuel Consumption of Motor Vehicles
(millions of gallons)

	Gasoline	Diesel	Total	Average km/gal
Guatemala	37.4	12.4	49.8	22.7
Honduras	14.6	7.3	21.9	14.8
El Salvador	19.3	7.3	26.6	29.4
Nicaragua	19.0	5.2	24.2	20.0
Costa Rica (1965)	18.8	13.4	32.2	22.2

8. The average American car does about 32 km per gallon on a tangent paved road. The figures above are lower than this but terrain is mountainous in most countries and trucks with a high fuel consumption account for a substantial part of the kilometers travelled. The lower figure for Honduras is consistent with the larger fraction of unpaved roads in that country.

9. The estimates above are the best that can be made with existing data. They are reasonably consistent with data on fuel consumption and vehicle registrations. On balance the number of vehicle kilometers may be underestimated.

TABLE 3.2:   Registration of Motor Vehicles in Central America, 1966

('000)

	Auto-mobiles	Cargo Vehicles	Bus	Jeeps and Station Wagons	Panels and Pickups	Total
Guatemala	29.6	6.7	2.9	12.9	9.4	61.5
Honduras[a]	10.6	6.7	1.5	[b]	[c]	18.8
El Salvador	22.2	3.4	2.2	[b]	12.8	40.6
Nicaragua	9.5	3.7	2.0	8.3	4.1	27.6
Costa Rica	16.2	4.5	2.1	10.9	7.8	41.5
Total	88.1	25.0	10.7	32.1	34.1	190.0
Percent	46	13	6	17	18	100

Source: Various government publications and documents.
Note: Data are somewhat unreliable for Honduras and Nicaragua where enforcement of vehicle registration does not reach outlying areas.
[a] Data for 1965.
[b] Included in automobiles.
[c] Included in cargo vehicles.

information available. There are approximately 67 people per vehicle in Central America, but the ratio varies considerably from country to country.[4]

Guatemala	71	people per vehicle
Honduras	125	" " "
El Salvador	71	" " "
Nicaragua	59	" " "
Costa Rica	33	" " "

Costa Rica with a higher per capita income over a sustained period and a more even distribution of income has less than half the number of people per vehicle than most of the other countries, while Honduras with the lowest per capita income has a significantly higher ratio.

The historical rate of growth of the vehicle population is difficult to estimate because improved data collection has given a large upward bias to the number of vehicles registered. Data on imports of vehicles indicate an average rate of growth of about 10 percent per year for total vehicle population. Only Costa Rica and Guatemala have data on the average age of vehicles (years):

	Costa Rica	Guatemala
Automobiles (incl. jeeps)	7.7	6
Trucks	8.4	7
Buses	7.9	6

[4] As of 1966. Some comparative data for other countries are as follows (people per vehicle): Argentina 17.5; Colombia 78.1; Brazil 43.7; Peru 51.5; Ecuador 123.5; Mexico 37.2; South America 36.9; United States 2.3; United Kingdom 5.3; (from U.N. Statistical Yearbook, 1965).

The average age of vehicles in Costa Rica is slightly higher than that of Guatemala because of the earlier growth of the vehicle population in Costa Rica and because higher import duties in Costa Rica encourage the repairing of old vehicles. In Honduras the average age of vehicles appears to be much lower because of low import duties, the more recent growth of the vehicle population and the poor quality of the road network.

A broad categorization of vehicle registration as of 1966 can be found in Table 3.2. It is difficult to obtain more detailed data on a comparable basis. Table 3.3 shows the distribution of the truck fleet in three countries.

TABLE 3.3: **Distribution of Cargo Vehicles (Excluding Pickups) in El Salvador (1964), Nicaragua (1966) and Costa Rica (1966)**

Capacity—Tons of Useful Cargo	El Salvador No.	El Salvador %	Nicaragua No.	Nicaragua %	Costa Rica No.	Costa Rica %
1 to 3	123	3	434	13	110	3
3 to 5	1,652	40	1,218	35	1,154	35
5 to 7	1,442	36	1,059	31	1,540	47
7 to 10	792	19	515	15	145	4
10 to 15	} 79	} 2	99	3	325	10
15 and above			105	3	34	1
Total	4,088	100	3,430	100	3,308	100

Source: El Salvador, Anuario Estadistico 1964, p. 383; Nicaragua, Highway Department. Costa Rica, Ministry of Transport, *Vehiculos Automotores en Circulacion*, September 1967, p. 72.

Note: Figures not directly comparable as definitions of capacity vary from country to country.

Most of the heavy trucks are in the range of 3 to 7 tons capacity. In Costa Rica "capacity" represents about 55 percent of gross weight. In Costa Rica 70 percent were diesel powered; in Guatemala the corresponding figure for heavy trucks was 25 percent.[5] In Costa Rica nine percent were tractor-trailer combinations with three or more axles. Information obtained from a survey made in 1966 in El Salvador for the purposes of estimating vehicle overloads, further reveals that the typical truck carries a load 59 percent greater than its rated capacity. (This overloading increases variable maintenance costs and thus should be reflected in the price charged for using the road—the EUC).

---

[5] In 1966 about 16,000 trucks were registered in Guatemala, 1,800 or 11 percent of which had diesel engines. The distribution of diesel engines differed widely between truck categories: 2% of light trucks, 25% of heavy trucks and 56% of tractor-trailers were of the diesel type. The combination of high diesel taxes and high license duties for trucks in Guatemala probably accounts for this large differential. In Costa Rica there are no diesel fuel taxes and license fees are low.

Railways and rail transport

The railways in Central America were built between 1870 and 1930 and located so as either to connect population centers with ports or to move banana exports. Design standards were limited and all lines are of narrow gauge which differs from line to line. The largest system, International Railways of Central America (IRCA), is privately owned and connects Guatemala City with the country's Atlantic and Pacific ports, San Salvador and the Mexican border—where, because of differing gauges, loads must be transferred. From San Salvador there are connections via the Ferrocarril de El Salvador to the Pacific port of Acajutla and to several points within the heavily populated regions of El Salvador. The other main system is in Costa Rica, where two different lines (one privately owned) connect the capital with the Atlantic and the Pacific. A small line exists in Nicaragua, and in Honduras three lines run along the Atlantic coast serving the banana trade.

Before the construction of the road network, these lines carried the bulk of all exports and imports; afterward they continued to carry substantial but declining proportions of this traffic.[6] As the highway network is completed and improved and the railroads lose their few remaining monopoly routes, the percentage of total traffic should become inconsequential. With one exception (El Salvador), the railroads are in financial difficulty and little hope can be held out that the situation will ever improve. Neither now nor in the foreseeable future will there be a significant demand for long hauls of bulk materials for which the railroads would be more suitable than highway transport. The only feasible alternative for most of the railroads is a gradual phasing out.[7]

Other forms of transport

Ports and shipping. Almost all of the region's trade with the world is handled through 30 ports on the Atlantic and Pacific coasts. The ports developed historically as part of the railroad network, which still operates the major ones in Guatemala, El Salvador, and Costa Rica. The tie of the ports to the railroad facilities has been a factor in maintaining railroad revenues and at the same time discouraging investment in road-connected port facilities. In Guatemala the railroad monopoly was broken by means of a parallel highway link to a new publicly-owned port. In most cases railroads have reacted slowly to a loss

---

[6] Volume of exports and imports carried by rail: Guatemala, exports 35 percent, imports 38 percent. El Salvador, exports 30 percent, imports 40 percent. Honduras, exports 60 percent, imports 20 percent.

[7] See IBRD Report WH–170a, Transport Appendix.

of their monopoly position and their failure to separate port charges from rail charges has resulted in an irrational structure for both.

Increases in international trade are placing a strong pressure on existing port facilities and all countries of the region are planning for major port expansion. These plans emphasize the importance of links to the highway network and the trend is likely to be one of increasing public ownership in the form of independent port authorities.

Other than a small public line in Guatemala, all international sea traffic is carried by ships of international firms. Little interregional trade takes place by means of coastal shipping. Inland waterways were once of great importance, but the navigational difficulties of the rivers combined with poor water connections between the main lakes has resulted in these waterways carrying only a very small proportion of the total traffic.

Airways and air transport. Poor domestic and international land routes resulted in the early development of air transport in Central America. Political and economic conditions (chiefly the lack of capital) have caused the larger commercial airlines to concentrate on the more profitable international routes, leaving the domestic traffic to small unscheduled operations. The pattern of operations is changing. Each country with the exception of El Salvador has a national public airline providing both national and international service. The introduction of jet aircraft with resulting increases in capacity threatens the profitability of the international traffic and may force some consolidation of airlines. Domestically, because of the short distances involved, the improvements in the highway network should diminish the role of internal air traffic.

The Pricing of Transport Services in Central America

It is difficult to find either a rational or consistent pattern in the pricing of transport services in Central America; policy appears to be a matter of historical accident rather than the result of conscious design. Recent studies have failed to emphasize the importance of this problem.[8] The formation of a common market is bringing the problem into sharper focus, however. The differences between national systems require some form of harmonization if the market is to work effectively. All the governments concerned have expressed considerable interest in this problem, although this interest has not as of the present extended itself to more overt action. Similar economies and a common historical tradition have resulted in remarkably similar policies towards pricing of the various modes of transport. This combined with the marginal importance of interregional trade has muted the pressures for change.

[8] See, for example, the TSC Report. This extensive report contains virtually no discussion of transport pricing for any mode of transport.

31

TABLE 3.4: The Interurban Road Budget, 1964

(million US$)

Country	User Taxes[a]	Road Costs[b]	Taxes as % of Costs
Guatemala	9.3	27.4	30
El Salvador	8.9	18.8	47
Honduras	2.2	10.1	22
Nicaragua	5.1	12.4	41
Costa Rica	6.1	15.8	39
Total	30.6	84.5	36

Source: IBRD Report No. WH–170a, *Economic Development and Prospects of Central America*, Vol. VI, Appendix A, p. 4.

[a] Total user charges with one-third deducted on the assumption they were paid by urban users.

[b] Defined as the total of the annual depreciation cost of the road system, the opportunity cost of invested capital, maintenance and administration costs.

Pricing of road services

Policy statements regarding the pricing of road services generally state that road users should pay their "fair" share or should cover the "costs" of roads. The economic basis for these policies has been questioned in the previous chapter, but even using this concept it is not apparent that it has been applied in practice. (See Table 3.4.)

It is obvious that using these estimates of costs and taxes, not only have the road users not come close to covering the costs of the roads but also that their so-called "fair" share will vary from country to country. El Salvadorian road users pay more than double the percentage of those of Honduras. Even altering the definition of road costs to exclude depreciation[9] does not change significantly the inter-country differences. It does, however, mean that users come closer to paying the full costs. (See Table 3.5.) In this case rural road users in El Salvador almost pay the full cost, and users in other countries come closer but still differ substantially from those of El Salvador. The concept is open to varying interpretations but even given an appropriate set of definitions their interpretation has varied in practice from country to country.

The essentially non-economic character of these policy statements is clearly evident when the actual system of user charges is examined. In El Salvador and Guatemala, for example, the taxes levied are very similar in their composi-

---

[9] This is done on the grounds that to include depreciation and maintenance is double counting costs. The assumption made in computing depreciation that the roads will be maintained so that they depreciate to zero value after 20 years seems unrealistic and contrary to the evidence available.

TABLE 3.5: The Interurban Road Budget, 1964, Excluding Depreciation

(million US$)

Country	User Taxes	Road Costs (*Minus Depreciation*)	Taxes as % of Costs
Guatemala	8.3	15.7	52.9
El Salvador	8.9	9.6	92.7
Honduras	2.2	5.7	38.6
Nicaragua	5.1	7.4	68.9
Costa Rica	6.1	8.3	73.5
Total	30.6	46.7	65.5

Source: IBRD Report No. WH–170a.

tion and level as well as their incidence in terms of vehicle kilometers. Yet by any concept of cost similar to the one illustrated above, Guatemalan road users pay half the proportion that those in El Salvador do. The conclusion that could be derived from this is that road charges should be doubled in Guatemala. This would then result in a situation in which it would cost twice the amount to move the same vehicle on the same type road in Guatemala than would be charged a few miles across the border in El Salvador, even though both the cost of using the road and the construction costs may be exactly equal. This type of conclusion appeals neither to common sense nor to economic theory.[10]

In practice, deviations from this interpretation of public policy seem to be closer to what would be dictated by a rational economic policy than that which would arise by a serious attempt to put stated policy into practice. Historical accident would appear to be better than bad theory.

Pricing of rail transport

Most of the railroad system[11] in Central America was developed by private capital, and as a result the influence of public policy on pricing of services has been only peripheral. This situation has gradually changed as railroads experienced financial difficulties and increasingly turned to the government for aid. Originally the railroads enjoyed a virtual monopoly over all import-export traffic and pricing policy took advantage of the situation. The effects of this monopoly power were mitigated by the fact that exporters held substantial interests in the railroads. In this period (roughly to 1950) government maintained its distance.

---

[10] It is even more difficult to accept this type of conclusion within the framework of a common market.

[11] The exception is the Ferrocarril al Pacífico in Costa Rica which began as a public enterprise. The Ferrocarril del Pacífico de Nicaragua has also been operated by the government over most of its existence.

33

At present the governments own four of the seven lines, but these four lines represent only 30 percent of the track. The lines in El Salvador, Nicaragua and Honduras have financial problems that are probably the result of the uneconomic character of these short-haul operations. Except for Honduras good parallel highway facilities are available. In Costa Rica the Ferrocarril al Pacífico operates with a balanced budget. Capital charges have been written off and the railroad tends to follow a system of marginal cost pricing, that is, of covering variable costs. At present this railroad is paralleled by a highway in poor condition. Truck operators seem convinced they could undercut the railroad if the (shorter) highway link were improved and if trucks were provided better access to the port. All of the public lines operate as independent agencies and the governments concerned have not attempted extensive rate regulation. Rate changes do, however, require some form of government approval.

The remaining three lines (four in practice as the El Salvador division of IRCA is operated independently of the Guatemalan division) still in private hands operate the major portion of the railroad network. One of these, the Northern Railway Co. in Costa Rica, still maintains a monopoly over its route, as a highway link between the capital and the Atlantic port of Limon is incomplete. Management of the line says the completion of the highway to Limon will not affect its revenue position. The bulk of revenues now come from the banana trade which uses an extensive system of railroad spurs for which at present there is no competing road network. How much of the profitability of the line is due to the monopoly position at the port is difficult to estimate because of the integrated nature of the operation.[12] The longest line in Central America (IRCA) operates in both El Salvador and Guatemala. It is experiencing serious financial difficulties with its Guatemalan division. The inability of management to adjust to the competition introduced by the building of a highway in the 1950's between Guatemala City and the Atlantic, combined with political and labor troubles, has left this railroad fighting for survival. Government has traditionally been hostile to the interests represented by the railroad management and has not always lent a sympathetic ear to the railroad's problems.[13] Some attempt has been made to aid the railroad by placing tolls on the parallel highway. This does not seem to have improved the situation. Management is free to set prices. Government approval is required, but it is more or less automatic. The El Salvador division of the railroad operates under a more dynamic management and seems to have adjusted to the changes

---

[12] Both the FEP and the Northern in Costa Rica charge lower port rates for those transporting by rail.

[13] See the Brookings Institution's Study on Impact of Atlantic Highway for a discussion of the railroad-government conflict during this period.

brought by improved highway transport. Rates are difficult to change, however, as they are included in the railroad's franchise and cannot be changed without opening the whole contract for negotiation. The remaining private line, the Tela Railroad, is operated by United Fruit Co. as part of its banana export business.

Public policy towards the railroads has been to more or less leave them alone.[14] The uneconomic character of most of the lines has been recognized by the governments and the main problem is how to phase them out. Governments have not attempted to set rates and in the face of railroad complaints about highway competition have turned a sympathetic but rather deaf ear.

Pricing of other forms of transport

Only port charges are of importance to land transport and this discussion will be limited to them.[15] The long coast lines of the Central American countries offer considerable potential for interregional coastal shipping, particularly if more development takes place along the coastal plains on both sides of the isthmus. Coastal shipping thus may become a potential competitor for highways in interregional trade of bulk commodities. In order for this trade to develop in an economic pattern where goods and services are carried by the lowest (economic) cost carrier, both highways and ports will have to be priced so as to reflect the real economic cost. This implies a reexamination of current pricing practices.

Even a casual examination of port charges in all Central American ports reveals the failure to apply any clear economic rationale. Most of the major ports started out as captive railroad ports where port and rail transport charges were essentially part of the same tariff. In many cases port charges compensated for railroad losses. The newer public ports (Matias de Galvez, Cortes and Acajutla) seem to have adopted virtually the same rate structure as existed in the railroad ports. No policy seems to exist with respect to competition between various ports. In Guatemala there are two nearby ports on the Atlantic, one a railroad port (Barrios) and the other (Matias de Galvez) served only by highway. After a period of competition both ports have established virtually the same rates.

There appears to be a need for considering port policy within the wider context of the common market. Improved interregional highway links and

---

[14] The railroads are exempt from most import duties and all fuel taxes.

[15] Public policy towards water and air transport is one of letting the market set the rate; in any case these have only a minor impact on road transport, the major focus of this study. It is conceivable, however, that if currently discussed plans of building an inland waterway along the Pacific coast are actually carried out, pricing for the services of this waterway will be of relevance.

an increasing volume of trade will bring previously non-competing ports into closer contact with one another, and this would seem the appropriate time to formulate a port pricing policy. As in the case of highways, the basis for this policy should be its effect on the allocation of resources.[16] A more rational system of pricing would also be of great assistance in making investment decisions for individual ports and within the context of a common market.

Revenues from Present User Taxes

Road user charges play an important role in revenue collections in at least four out of the five countries of Central America. In 1966 road taxes contributed the following to total central government revenues. (For details see Table 3.9, p. 44.)

			(million US$)
	User Taxes	*Current Revenues*	*Taxes as % of Revenues*
Guatemala	17.4	121.0	14
El Salvador	11.8	89.5	13
Honduras	3.6	60.2	6
Nicaragua	6.0	66.6	9
Costa Rica	10.1	77.6	13

The contribution of road taxes to public revenues appears to be of considerable importance in all countries except Honduras, where the vehicle population is much smaller relative to the size of the road network. Their contribution is roughly the same percentage as that of direct taxes (again with the exception of Honduras).

About 60 percent of the revenues collected come from fuel taxes alone. Vehicle purchase taxes in the form of both import and sales taxes account for an additional 20 to 25 percent with most of the remainder coming from license fees. (See Table 3.6.)

Quasi-Tax Elements of Highway Transport Costs[17]

In addition to private operating costs and user taxes there are various costs imposed either by market imperfections or government policy. If these costs are

---

[16] In recent years the port pricing and investment problem has been widely discussed. See, for example, R. O. Goss, "Economic Appraisal of Port Investment," *Journal of Transport Economics and Policy* (September, 1967) pp. 249–72.

[17] See Table 3.7. p. 42.

TABLE 3.6:   Road Taxes, Revenues Collected and Percentage Composition, 1966

(million US$)

	Fuel Taxes		Import Sales & Tires		License Fees		Tolls		Total
	US$	%	US$	%	US$	%	US$	%	US$
Guatemala	10.0	57	4.5	26	2.6	15	0.3	2	17.4
El Salvador	6.6	56	3.6	30	1.6	14	–	–	11.8
Honduras	2.1	58	0.9	25	0.6	17	–	–	3.6
Nicaragua	2.7	45	2.6	43	0.7	12	–	–	6.0
Costa Rica	6.2	61	2.3	23	1.3	13	0.3	3	10.1

the result of government policy they may be regarded as a form of taxation, but it is usually a form of taxation that is difficult to quantify. For purposes of simplifying the analysis, this study considers these quasi-tax elements as a separate part of the pricing problems. This division of the problem is in effect establishing an analytical framework of two parts; one part in which no ceteris paribus assumptions are made and one part in which pricing is considered given certain assumptions about the economy. This is done for a very simple reason—it still makes sense to talk about pricing regardless of the distortions that can arise from what can be termed the quasi-tax elements; that is, resource allocation can be maximized within a given set of constraints. The taxes and charges imposed on road users are discussed in Chapter V. The assumption made in the discussion of these taxes is that the economic and institutional framework is given and that the problem is one of pricing within the constraints of this framework. It is not necessary, however, to accept all of the elements of the framework as given. Certain elements have an obviously adverse effect upon the efficient allocation of resources, particularly within the transport sector, and at the same time are amenable to change through government action. These elements can be found in all modes of transport, but only the more important ones in highway transport are discussed below.

Border crossing procedures

Excessive border crossing costs are by far the single most distortive element in the present system of pricing road transport. According to the implementation schedules, tariff walls within the Common Market will virtually be eliminated by 1970; unless border crossing procedures are improved, however, free trade in an important number of commodities will be far from being achieved in practice. Slow and inefficient border crossing procedures can be an effective substitute for tariffs. At present these procedures add substantially to transport costs by a combination of excessive delays, lengthy administrative procedures (such as unloading of vehicles), and inconvenient hours of operation. Personnel and facilities have not been expanded to meet the growing volume of traffic, with the result that the costs of increased delays have to some extent substituted for lower tariffs.

These costs are difficult to quantify exactly because of the variations encountered for types of cargo, trucks and border posts. The following estimate is of costs which might be considered typical. According to trucking firms interviewed, average delay time at the frontiers of all the countries amounts to from three to five hours. They estimate their costs at between $8 and $10 per hour (costs of capital, labor, overhead, etc.). To this must be added discharging costs of approximately $3 per truck[18] and in some cases an additional $3 to $12 for speeding up the process of documentation.[19] Thus the costs for taking a medium size truck across a frontier range on the average from between $40 and $60.

The table below shows the impact of these border costs on the cost of transportation between Guatemala City and San Salvador in different types of trucks. In all cases the border costs raise total transport costs between 200 and 300 percent. In Table 3.8 (p. 43) an attempt is made to estimate the effects of these transportation charges on the price of some commodities typically traded in Central America. The commodities selected are those with a high bulk in relation to their value, that is, those in which transport costs would have their greatest impact. These commodities account for a substantial part of interregional trade. The implied "tariffs" resulting from the high cost of border crossing are by no means trivial:

	Border Crossing Cost per Ton as % of c.i.f. Price per Ton	*Previous Ad Valorem Tariff Guatemala, El Salvador, Honduras*	
Cement	20	(5)	
Lumber	9	(8)	
Beans	4		
Maize	7	(59)	(55)
Sugar			
Refined	4		
Raw	8		
Fertilizers	12	(17)	
Fruits and Vegetables	7		
Maicillo	6		

---

[18] Truckers cannot load or unload their own vehicles but must use labor provided by customs officials.

[19] These fees do not go into government revenues. In Guatemala they are 40 cents per signature.

In some cases they represent a higher barrier to interregional trade than previously existing tariffs.

The above costs refer only to the crossing of one border; were these commodities to be traded between more distant Central American countries where more than one border was crossed, the costs would increase proportionally. The suspicion that this kind of protection is almost prohibitive for high bulk low value items is given added confirmation by the fact that very little trade in these items does take place. Most of the trade between the extreme ends of the Common Market is in the form of higher value manufactured products for consumption and industry. This is not, of course, exclusively the result of border crossing costs but also of high transport costs per se. The elimination of border crossing costs could result in a substantial increase in Central American trade of certain commodities, particularly the low value high bulk type mentioned above. For a number of commodities third countries supply an important part of total imports. These could be replaced by Central American supplies if border crossing "tariffs" were eliminated. For example, El Salvador buys about one-fourth of total imported cement from third countries (Colombia, Germany). Eliminating border crossing costs would reduce the price of Honduran and Guatemalan cement by about 20 percent, which might be enough to give preference to the Central American suppliers. A similar case is grain imports from third countries into Central America. While in 1965 El Salvador and Guatemala were meeting most of their internal corn shortage by imports from Honduras, both Costa Rica and Nicaragua were mainly importing from the U.S. or from Mexico. This is not surprising since transport costs of Honduran corn (of which a substantial part are border crossing costs) would be prohibitively high, amounting to over 50 percent of the demand price for corn in Costa Rica. Again, an elimination of border crossing costs could shift part or all of the Nicaraguan and Costa Rican import demand for corn to Central American suppliers.[20] Given the magnitudes of border crossing costs it appears conceivable that their elimination could reduce the supply prices of quite a number of (bulk) commodities below those of competitive third country imports and hence make the demand for Central American supplies very elastic.

In some cases movement across intermediate countries can be made cheaper by sealing or bonding the vehicle. Costs are not, however, negligible. If a truck can be sealed, passage through El Salvador and Guatemala is possible,

---

[20] The *Special Protocol on Grains* which was agreed upon by the Central American countries in 1966 is designed to work in the same direction. It eliminates all trade barriers for basic grains within Central America and increases the price of third country grain imports to the level of Central American supplies.

but in the other countries a customs guard is required to accompany the vehicle whether or not it is sealed. Rates for customs guards are as follows (US$ per trip):

Guatemala	$ 20.00
El Salvador	40.00
Honduras	9.50
Nicaragua	10.00
Costa Rica	10.00
Panama	75.00

Trucks thus bonded escape some of the waiting time at the frontier but not all of it.

Additional barriers to interregional trade can be found in the licensing requirements of each country. A truck can haul between points in two different countries, but it cannot pick up and deliver in a country other than the one in which it is registered. Thus a truck with Salvadorian registry can carry a load from San Salvador to San Pedro Sula in Honduras and from there to Managua in Nicaragua. It cannot, however, pick up freight in San Pedro Sula and make an intermediate delivery in Tegucigalpa, Honduras without having registered in Honduras and paying the necessary import duties. This registration is in the form of an annual license fee. The higher this license the greater the protection given locally registered vehicles. The effect of these licensing regulations cannot be estimated from existing data. A preferable system would be a system of temporary licenses granted on a trip basis.

Domestic fuel refining and distribution

An important element in the taxation of road users in Central America is the tax on fuels. The actual taxes levied are not entirely representative of the tax burden imposed upon consumers. Consumers in effect are also subject to the implicit tax involved in the protection of inefficient domestic refining operations. The Central American countries have developed mini-refineries which are well below the most efficient size. While it is impossible to determine exactly what increase in costs results and how much of this is borne by consumers, it appears that its impact on transport costs is small.

In addition consumers are subject to the increased prices of fuels resulting from the cartelization of the marketing channels. A complex structure of prices exists for fuels in Central America depending upon the geographical location of the market outlet. This structure does not reflect the differential costs of supply and as a consequence an implied tax burden is placed on some consumers. While this burden is not excessive, neither is it negligible.

Domestic tire production

The same general considerations apply in the case of the price of tires as in the case of oil refining. Since 1962 part of the domestic demand for tires has been met by domestic production of tires from two firms. The level of protection given to domestic production is approximately 40 percent and it appears that this is being fully exploited. Both plants are high cost operations.

TABLE 3.7: Tax and Quasi-Tax Elements of Road Transport Costs for Typical Vehicles[a]

(cents per veh/km and per ton/km)

	18-Ton Truck Diesel			7-Ton Truck Gasoline			1-Ton Truck Gasoline	
	Per veh/km	Per ton/km	Cumulative %	Per veh/km	Per ton/km	Cumulative %	Per veh/km and Per ton/km	Cumulative %
1) Private Operating Costs (ex taxes)	9.41	.52		6.94	.99		3.91	
2) Variable Road Maintenance Costs	.10	.00		.10	.01		.10	
3) Sub-Total (1 + 2)	9.51	.52	100	7.04	1.00	100	4.01	100
4) User Charges Exceeding EUC's	.70	.04	107	2.34	.33	133	1.17	129
5) Difference Domestic and World Market Tire Prices	.38	.02	111	.13	.02	135	.04	130
6) Difference Domestic and World Market Fuel Refining Price	.06	.00	112	.12	.02	137	.05	131
7) Sub-Total (3 + 4 + 5 + 6)	10.65	.58	112	9.63	1.37	137	5.27	131
8) Border Crossing Costs	21.23	1.18	320	15.83	2.26	363	10.03	381
Total	31.88	1.76	320	25.46	3.63	363	15.30	381

7-ton truck: 4-hour waiting time, $8 per hour, $3 discharging vehicle, $6 signing customs papers.
1-ton truck: 4-hour waiting time $5 per hour, $3 discharging vehicle, $3 signing customs papers.

[a] Running on paved roads between San Salvador and Guatemala City (259 km). Vehicle licensed in Guatemala. Speed 80 km/hr.

Sources and Assumptions:
1) De Weille, pp. 45–77, adjusted for local prices.
2) Chapter IV, p. 46.
4) Table 5.9.
5) Goodyear (ex-import duty) and GINSA price lists.
6) Estimated 2¢ per gallon of gasoline and 1¢ per gallon of diesel.
8) 18-ton truck: 4-hour waiting time $10 per hour, $12 for signing of customs papers, $3 for discharging vehicle.

TABLE 3.8: Incidence of Tax and Quasi-Tax Elements in Transport Prices on Typical Low-Value Commodities Traded within Central America

					Tax and Quasi-Tax Price Elements							
					$ Per Ton				% of Unit Value			
	Exp. from	Imp. into	Volume transp. '000 mt.	Unit value $/ton	Average distance transp. km	User charges	Cost of domestic tires	Cost of domestic gas ref.	Border crossing costs	UC	T	G	B
	(1)		(2)	(3)	(4)	(5)	(6)	(7)	(8)	(9)	(10)	(11)	(12)
Cement	H	ES	45	29	400	1.52	.08	.08	5.80	3.4	0	0	20.0
	G	ES	23	29	260	.99	.03	.03	5.80	5.2	0	0	20.0
Lumber	H	ES	55	64	360	1.36	.07	.07	5.80	2.1	0	0	9.0
Beans	H	ES	23	154	250	.60	.05	.05	5.80	.3	0	0	3.8
Corn	H	ES	65	85	250	.60	.05	.05	5.80	.7	0	0	6.8
Sugar													
Refined	ES	H	4	143	360	1.36	.07	.07	5.80	1.0	0	0	3.5
Raw	ES	H	3	77	360	1.36	.07	.07	5.80	1.8	0	0	7.5
Fertilizers	ES	G	13	49	260	.91	.03	.03	5.80	1.8	0	0	11.8
Fruits and Veg.	G	ES	44	82	260	.91	.03	.03	5.80	1.1	0	0	7.1
Sorghum	H	ES	2	93	250	.60	.05	.05	5.80	.6	0	0	6.2

Sources: Cols. (2), (3): Trade Statistics; Col. (5): Table 5.9; Cols. (6), (7), (8): Table 3.7.

G—Guatemala; H—Honduras; ES—El Salvador.

Assumption: The goods are transported by a 7-ton gasoline truck.

Average distance transported is taken either between capitals or, where known, between production center and capital. Unit values according to trade statistics.

TABLE 3.9: Revenue Collected from Road User Taxes as Compared to Central Government Current Revenues, 1964–66

(million US$)

| | | User Taxes | | | | Total Current Revenues (6) | (5) as % of (6) (7) |
		Fuel Taxes (1)	Import Duties or Sales Taxes on Vehicles and Parts (2)	License Fees (3)	Tolls (4)	Total (5)		
Guatemala	1963/1964	6.8	3.9	1.7	n.a.	12.4	104.0	11.9
	1965	5.8	4.9	2.4	0.3	13.4	121.5	11.0
	1966	10.0	4.5	2.6	0.3	17.4	121.0	14.4
El Salvador	1964	4.2	2.9	1.2	–	8.3	81.7	10.2
	1965	6.5	3.1	1.5	–	11.1	89.5	12.4
	1966	6.6	3.6	1.6	–	11.8	89.1	13.2
Honduras	1964	2.2	0.7	0.4	–	3.3	46.5	7.0
	1965	2.4	0.8	0.5	–	3.7	54.9	6.7
	1966	2.1	0.9	0.6	–	3.6	60.2	5.9
Nicaragua	1964	n.a.	1.7	.3	–	6.7	54.3	n.a.
	1965	2.5	2.5	.4	–	5.4	64.2	8.4
	1966	2.7	2.6	.7	–	6.0	66.0	9.0
Costa Rica	1964	4.5	3.2	.9	–	8.6	65.6	13.1
	1965	5.0	2.2	.9	.1	8.2	71.8	11.4
	1966	6.2	2.3	1.3	.3	10.1	77.6	13.0

Source: IBRD Report, WH-170a, Economic Development and
Prospects of Central America and Government sources.

IV

COST AND INVESTMENTS

Maintenance Costs

No general consensus exists as to the desirable level of maintenance expenditures for various classes of roads. At best there are general guidelines—such as the U.S. Bureau of Public Roads suggestion of about $800 a year per mile of paved road in order to maintain the road in its "original state." Such a maintenance expenditure might be described as the standard maintenance cost since it specifies precisely the ("as before") state of the road after maintenance. From an economic point of view this standard maintenance expenditure is not necessarily ideal or optimum. It may be better to have lower than standard maintenance expenditures if, for example, the road is to be reconstructed in a few years, or the benefits to the traffic using the road are less than the maintenance expenditures.[1]

In practice considerable variations will be found between standard (or ideal) and actual maintenance expenditures. There are lags and leads in maintenance spending, so that the expenditures in any given period may not accurately reflect the average. Also the maintenance program may be subject to budgetary or political pressures rather than being the end-product of a more narrowly defined economic calculation. Probably more important than either of these factors is the heterogeneity of highways—some in mountainous areas

---

[1] This is really part of the investment decision, see pp. 20–22.

TABLE 4.1: Average Maintenance Costs per Kilometer per Year

(US$)

	Guatemala	Honduras	El Salvador	Nicaragua	Costa Rica
Paved Roads	843	784	1,027	1,657	1,420
Gravel Roads	489	571	336	–	–
Earth Roads	–	–	274	–	–

are subject to falls, etc. whereas others are on flat well-drained land and are much cheaper to maintain.

Table 4.1 shows some of the variation in maintenance costs per kilometer of road in Central America. These averages were obtained from a sample of maintenance expenditures for individual stretches of road in each country. Not all of the data is of the same quality. One of the major problems is to separate maintenance expenditures from those made for improvement or upgrading. In this respect the data for Costa Rica and Guatemala are most suspect. Accounts are not kept on a per road basis, nor are adequate distinctions made between capital and maintenance expenditures. The average for Nicaragua is probably a fairly accurate reflection of maintenance expenditures. Maintenance expenditures are budgeted separately from capital expenditures and detailed records are kept on a road by road basis for the main highway network. The average of 1,657 dollars per kilometer was obtained over a three-year period (1964–67). In El Salvador only expenditures on labor for maintenance purposes are kept on a road by road basis. Maintenance expenditures on machinery, fuel, etc., were estimated by weighting the total expenditure by the labor component of each road. The data are only for one year but the sample is large and covers most of the country's road network. The averages for Honduras are based on two years of data that appear to be of good quality.

Some of the difference in expenditures from country to country can be accounted for by such factors as terrain, traffic volume, etc. but most of the difference is due to the different standards of maintenance. Nicaragua's highways are kept in better condition than those of El Salvador or Guatemala. The high average figure for Costa Rica does not indicate high maintenance standards but simply the inclusion of some construction expenditures.

Variable maintenance costs

In order to set a price equal to the economic user charge it is necessary to have some idea of the magnitude of the maintenance costs that vary with traffic volume. Roads with higher traffic volume should have higher maintenance costs. These costs known as the variable maintenance costs (VMC) will

46

be a function of the volume of traffic, the type of traffic, and the class of road. It should be possible by correlating these factors to obtain an estimate of the variable maintenance costs.

The last of these factors, the class of road, can be handled statistically by considering roads of a homogeneous class as one set and then estimating the *VMC* for each set. Because of the quality of the data, it has not been possible to consider other than a very broad classification of road types. The best that can be done is to divide roads into three categories, paved, gravel and earth. The distinction between paved and unpaved roads is fairly clear but the classification of unpaved roads is subject to some confusion. The difference between an earth road and a gravel road is often a matter of degree rather than a matter of a fine dividing line. These rough divisions are not entirely satisfactory; it would be preferable to classify paved roads by, for example, depth of paving, gravel roads by the size of the aggregate, etc. Fortunately for purposes of establishing the level of the economic user charge these distinctions are not very important. The instruments for collecting these charges are so blunt that fine distinctions have to be ignored. In any case the evidence available suggests that the biggest differences in costs occur between classes of surfaces (paved-gravel) rather than between types in the same class (asphalt-concrete).

The second factor, the type of traffic, is a more difficult problem to deal with statistically. If variable maintenance costs vary with the type of traffic, or to be more precise by the weight per axle of a vehicle, the expectation would be that in the case of two roads with the same number of vehicles the maintenance costs would be higher if one of these roads carried a higher proportion of heavy vehicles. To obtain an estimate of the maintenance costs attributable to the passage of heavy vehicles would require a small sample with large variations in the proportion of heavy and light vehicles or a large sample with smaller variations. It was not possible to do this in Central America because the samples of homogeneous sets of roads are small and the proportion of light to heavy vehicles is roughly similar on all roads.[2]

The division between light and heavy vehicles is, of course, only part of the problem. It would be desirable for purposes of levying economic user charges to know the variable maintenance costs caused by a five-ton truck. No definitive conclusions on this question are immediately available but what evidence does

---

[2] Regressing maintenance costs on volume of heavy traffic merely reflects the proportion of heavy traffic to total traffic. This high correlation between heavy and light vehicle flow effectively renders otiose any attempt to conduct a multiple regression analysis.

exist, together with the opinions of informed observers, suggest that damage done to roads by vehicles is a function of their weight.[3]

The results: paved roads

Only in El Salvador and Nicaragua[4] was it possible to obtain sufficient data that combined traffic counts and maintenance costs for the same stretches of road. The regression of maintenance costs on ADT gave the following results:

$$\text{Annual Maintenance Costs on Paved Roads (\$ per km)} = 1{,}219 + 0.37 \text{ ADT } \textit{Nicaragua}$$

$$\text{Annual Maintenance Costs on Paved Roads (\$ per km)} = 520 + 0.48 \text{ ADT } \textit{El Salvador}$$

As is to be expected with cross-section data of this kind, the coefficient of correlation is small ($r = +0.32$ in Nicaragua and $r = +0.61$ in El Salvador) and in the case of Nicaragua the standard error of the regression estimate is high (0.21) but reasonable in El Salvador (0.14). It is proposed, however, to interpret the figures, to compare them with similar data, and then to assess the statistical validity of the interpretation.

A simple interpretation is that the authorities must spend $1,219 per annum in Nicaragua and $520 per annum in El Salvador to maintain a paved road even though no traffic uses it. For every additional vehicle in the average daily vehicle flow on the road the authorities must spend 37 cents per year per kilometer in Nicaragua and 48 cents per year per kilometer in El Salvador. Thus an additional vehicle kilometer involves the authorities in an additional expenditure of 0.10 cents in Nicaragua and 0.13 cents in El Salvador. The results suggest that with paved roads by far the largest fraction of maintenance expenditure is independent of the traffic volume. Only if the vehicle count is above 3,000 or so in Nicaragua and above 1,100 in El Salvador do aggregate variable maintenance expenditures exceed the fixed maintenance costs. This occurred for only two roads of the sample of 28 in Nicaragua and for eight roads of the sample of 22 in El Salvador.

An interesting feature that calls for some explanation is the large difference in fixed maintenance costs between the two countries. (See Table 4.2.) Average daily traffic volumes are roughly equal in both cases: 1049 in El Salvador and 1198 in Nicaragua. The reason for this difference must lie

---

[3] The AASHO Road Test (National Research Council, Publication No. 816 Washington, D.C., 1961) does not define its concepts in economic terms and it was not possible to use this data to estimate variable maintenance costs.

[4] Some data were obtained in Costa Rica but were unusable because of the problem of distinguishing improvement from maintenance costs.

TABLE 4.2: Highway Network and Maintenance Expenditures, Nicaragua and El Salvador

(in kilometers and million US$)

	Nicaragua	El Salvador
Paved Roads	878	1,058
Gravel Roads	2,263	2,024
Earth Roads	3,550	5,447
Total	6,691	8,529
Approx. Annual Maintenance Expend.	2.4	2.0
Maintenance Expenditures per km	260	230

either in the physical terrain or in the different standards according to which the roads are maintained. The terrain, types of road, (width, design standards, etc.) are roughly similar; the more probable reason is that roads in El Salvador are maintained at a lower standard than those of Nicaragua. This is the opinion of most informed observers and is obvious in the aggregate figure of maintenance expenditures. The higher variable maintenance costs in El Salvador might also be the result of the lower maintenance standards. Variable maintenance costs tend to be inversely related to the quality of the road.[5]

---

[5] This apparent paradox is easily settled if all maintenance expenditures are considered part of the investment decision. Thus in some cases it may be more economic to maintain a road at a lower standard with a higher EUC than at a higher standard with a low EUC. The costs of maintaining the higher standards may exceed the benefits.

The relation of maintenance costs to the quality of the road may also mean that the regression coefficient obtained from the data may not correctly represent the true marginal cost. This is the marginal cost of additional service of the same quality, or if quality necessarily changes, the cost incurred in carrying additional traffic less an allowance for the value of any concurrent improvement in the quality of service obtained by the existing traffic (or plus the value of any deterioration). If maintenance standards are generally higher on road segments of higher ADT, and thus result in higher quality service and lower operating costs (e.g., due to an adjustment for quality), this would mean that the regression coefficient obtained from the data would overstate marginal cost.

If on the other hand high traffic roads are maintained at a higher level, either by more expensive original construction specifications or by earlier application of maintenance expenditures (not for the sake of a higher quality of service but because the future maintenance savings are less remote and less heavily discounted), then the lower marginal maintenance costs might have to be offset by including more of the capital charges in marginal cost. Much depends on whether the sampled roads contain appropriate proportions of recently constructed roads for which maintenance would tend to be light in the low traffic segments, but closer to the long-run norm in the high-traffic segments. In any case this is a refinement of concept that exceeds what the available data will support.

These results can be compared with those obtained by other studies. Because of the similarity of technology in the provision of road services, it would be surprising to find substantial differences in costs from country to country. The U.S. Bureau of Public Roads suggests that maintenance costs per kilometer on paved roads are about $800 to $900 per annum but does not attempt to estimate the variation with traffic flow. The average expenditures on maintenance in Guatemala and Honduras fall within this range, but it is doubtful whether these roads would ever be considered as being well maintained. Soberman in his study of Venezuela found the following results for paved roads:[6]

$$\text{Annual Maintenance Costs on Paved Roads (\$ per km)} = 2,300 + 0.2\,\text{ADT}$$

Clearly such figures suggest that invariate maintenance expenditure is very high indeed and variable maintenance cost is very low—only 20 cents compared with the Central American estimates of 37 and 48 cents per year per ADT-km. That Soberman's estimates are too low may also be adduced from the experience of the Road Research Laboratory of the United Kingdom, where it was suggested that about one cent per vehicle mile (or 0.6 cents per vehicle kilometer) was an appropriate figure for variable maintenance cost.[7] These data are not inconsistent with the Central American results which are higher than Soberman's.

Yet another check is available from the data collected by the Louisiana Highway Department.[8] This study of 288 observations was sufficiently detailed so as to enable the authors to extract what might be termed "nuisance" variables[9]—such as surface condition, sub-soil condition, surface width, right of way width, etc. The results are, however, not quite comparable to those

[6] Richard M. Soberman, "Economic Analysis of Highway Design in Developing Countries." Highway Research Board, *Highway Record*, No. 115, Publication 1337, 1966.

[7] Report of the Committee on Road Pricing (The Smeed Report) Appendix 2. H.M.S.O. London (1965). The Road Research Laboratory figure (0.6 vehicle km) is not supported by any evidence but is merely an educated "guess." It appears to be on the high side possibly due to the conditions existing in the U.K.— heavy traffic volumes, high maintenance standards, and the fact that a large part of the road network is urban with additional maintenance costs (drainage, traffic control, etc.).

[8] Z. K. Sutarwala and L. Mann, "A Formula for the Allocation of Maintenance Funds for Highways using a Mathematical Model to Predict Maintenance Costs." *Engineering Experiment Station Bulletin No. 72*. Louisiana State University, Baton Rouge (1963).

[9] See below.

obtained in Central America as they apply to concrete pavements which may
be less susceptible to vehicle damage than asphalt carpets. Nevertheless, the
Louisiana data show that an increase of one vehicle per day increases the
annual maintenance costs by 0.49 dollars a mile. Thus a vehicle kilometer
causes damages of about 0.08 cents. This evidence, although indirect and
inferential, does not suggest that the figures obtained for Central America are
discredited. In light of this and other evidence, an annual variable maintenance
cost of between 37 and 48 cents per unit ADT per kilometer or 0.10 to 0.13
cents a vehicle kilometer appears as reasonable an estimate as can be made
with existing data.

The results: unpaved roads

The results for unpaved roads are a good deal more unsatisfactory than
those for paved roads. Roads of this type are often local roads on which
accurate maintenance accounts are not usually kept, and traffic counts taken
only on a sporadic basis. In addition there is a serious identification problem;
there is generally no sharp distinction between earth and gravel roads but
rather a continuous gradient of quality. Only in El Salvador was it possible
to obtain for one year maintenance costs and associated traffic volumes classified
into ballasted (gravel) roads and unballasted (earth) roads. Attempts to
correlate maintenance expenditures with traffic volumes yielded no significant
results. This is not surprising given the poor quality of the maintenance data,
the traffic counts, and the rather vague classification of road surfaces and
conditions.

Evidence on costs for these types of surfaces must thus come from other
sources. Soberman's study on Venezuela yielded the following results:[10]

$$\text{Annual Maintenance Costs (\$ per km)} = 1{,}150 + 4.0 \, \text{ADT} \quad Gravel$$

$$\text{Annual Maintenance Costs (\$ per km)} = 344 + 12.0 \, \text{ADT} \quad Earth$$

Transformed into variable maintenance costs these relationships become 1.1
cents a kilometer on gravel surfaces and 3.3 cents on earth surfaces.

Additional data on unpaved roads in Africa suggests that these magnitudes
are not unreasonable. The following are for gravel (Kenya) and laterite
(Congo) surfaces:[11]

---

[10] Soberman, "Economic Analysis of Highway Design. . . ."
[11] Kenya data from British Road Research Laboratory East Africa Transport
Planning Research Unit, *A Study of Road Maintenance Costs in Kenya.* Mimeograph, 1966. Congo data from F. Soges.

51

$$\text{Annual Maintenance Costs} \atop (\$ \text{ per km}) \quad = \quad 168 + 2.4 \text{ ADT} \quad Gravel$$

$$\text{Annual Maintenance Costs} \atop (\$ \text{ per km}) \quad = \quad 270 + 5.3 \text{ ADT} \quad Laterite$$

Substantial differences between the African and Venezuelan data are to be noted in the fixed component. This may be due largely to climatic factors, principally rainfall. The variable components are, however, of roughly the same magnitude; 0.6 cents per vehicle kilometer on gravel roads in Kenya and 1.4 on laterite roads in the Eastern Congo. The apparently low figure for Kenya can probably be explained by the fact that the estimate is on the basis of grants to administrative districts rather than on the relationship of actual expenditures and traffic volumes. These results give added support to the hypothesis that the variable maintenance costs on gravel roads are approximately ten times those of a paved road. For earth roads the figure must be higher; the Venezuelan data indicate that the costs are thirty times those of a paved road. There are no reasons to doubt that the cost differentials in Central America are of a similar order of magnitude.

Interpretation of the results

With the elimination of this source of variance the estimate of the variable maintenance costs would be different. How much is difficult to estimate. The results obtained are an average: with the elimination of the variance due to different road types the variable maintenance costs might be higher on some roads (e.g. in mountainous terrain) than others. Available evidence suggests that this difference, if it exists at all, is not likely to be very large.

In the case of the Nicaraguan data it is possible to eliminate one source of variation. The estimated equation on page 48 was obtained by counting as individual observations the two sets of traffic and maintenance statistics for the years 1965 and 1966. Clearly maintenance expenditure is not a continuous process and considerable year-to-year variations may be encountered for any given stretch of road. Part of this effect can be eliminated by averaging traffic flow and average maintenance expenditure on each road. The regression equation was:

$$\text{Annual Maintenance Cost} \atop (\$ \text{ per km}) \quad = \quad 1{,}071 + 0.44 \text{ ADT}$$

The correlation coefficient was (for cross-section results) relatively high ($r = 0.47$) and the standard error of the regression coefficient (0.22) is not as large as in the original data.[12] These figures suggest that the variable main-

[12] For those who put their faith in significance tests; at the 95 percent level the "experimental" $r = 1.915$ falls just short of the theoretical to .95 = 2.145.

tenance costs are somewhat higher than indicated in the original data: an addition of one vehicle to the ADT adds about 44 cents to the kilometer cost of maintenance, and this is approximately 0.12 cents a vehicle kilometer. The difference is small but the results are closer to those of El Salvador which are of a more selective nature. The rise in the "goodness of fit" of the regression does suggest that there is some substantive evidence supporting the heterogeneity arguments.

This point can be examined further by considering only roads of a more or less homogeneous quality where the authority attains about the standard maintenance expenditure; that is, all roads are maintained to more or less the same standard.[13] This means that new roads which have been open only a few months would have to be excluded as maintenance expenditures should be very low. (If we do this, however, capital charges would have to be reduced by the amortization made possible out of the low maintenance costs of the first few years.) Similarly maintenance expenditures might be low on roads which are to be reconstructed or improved in the near future, and thus should also be excluded. It was possible to exclude new or reconstructed roads as well as roads for which major improvements were planned in the data for El Salvador. The estimating equation above on page 48 is based on an original sample of 36 observations, 14 of which were excluded. Before this was done the results were not statistically significant. The elimination of eight of the most obvious of the observations pertaining to roads which were either new or about to be constructed was sufficient to yield significant results. The regression with eight instead of fourteen observations omitted was as follows:

$$\text{Annual Maintenance Cost (\$ per km)} \quad = \quad 711 + 0.34\,\text{ADT}$$

The correlation coefficient was relatively high ($r = 0.41$) and the standard error of the regression coefficient quite small (0.15). The variable maintenance cost would then be 0.09 cents a vehicle kilometer.

Unfortunately the description of roads in Nicaragua was not as precise as that for El Salvador and it was not possible to make an a priori selection of observations to be omitted. If, however, only the roads described as "good" by the authorities are included in the analysis, the sample of roads should be fairly homogeneous because new roads (described as "very good" or "excellent") and the deteriorating roads (described as "fair" or "poor" or "bad") would be excluded. Using again the average figures for the two years, the

---

[13] Whether this is a desirable standard from the point of view of economic efficiency is another question.

scatter of maintenance expenditures for good roads could be plotted. The first point of interest would be that there are fewer observations (6) than in the overall analysis. Nevertheless, a regression fitted to these observations of the good roads would clearly suggest that the orders of magnitude found with the overall regression are not discredited by the analysis of only the "good" roads. The size of both the slope and the intercepts would be roughly the same.

Summary

The search for a systematic relationship between the volume of traffic and the expenditure on maintenance has been the main purpose of this section. All the data revealed a positive correlation between the two variables. But, judged by the ordinary statistical tests, the correlations were low (at the normal 95 percent levels) and in some cases not inconsistent with a zero value. It is possible to ascribe some of this variation in the data to the inherent characteristics of the cross-section roads, and the small correlations are due partly to this "road-variation" rather than variations from one sample to another. Undoubtedly, however, much of the fuzziness in the data is due to the fact that the maintenance costs for a particular year reflect the great variations from one year to another; deferments and lumpiness of maintenance are important. Some measure of the effect appeared in the estimates for Nicaragua where a marked improvement in the correlation occurred when the data for two years were aggregated. Smoothing out the annual vagaries of maintenance expenditure would add to the degree of systematic explanation.

The estimates of the values of the coefficients of variable maintenance costs were not inconsistent with those obtained in other studies. There is good reason to believe that because of the "regression fallacy" that there is a downward bias in those estimated.[14] The true coefficients of variable maintenance costs are likely to be higher than those that emerged from the regression equations. How much higher is an unanswerable question, but an upper limit might be a doubling of the estimate—from 0.1 cents to 0.2 cents a vehicle kilometer. Unfortunately the data could not be used to estimate the variable maintenance costs of different types of vehicles—particularly heavy trucks. The evidence that is available suggests that damage to roads is related to axle

---

[14] The effect of random variations in traffic flow, or of systematic supply responses (high traffic one year leading to high maintenance expenditures the next year), will flatten out the statistical observations. The observed coefficient of variable maintenance costs will be too low. A controlled experiment has not been performed. ADT is a random variable, that is, it is not fixed. Errors in measuring the ADT's *in addition* to the errors in measuring the maintenance costs give a least squares estimator that, on the average, is biased downwards.

54

weight.[15] Data was also of insufficient quality to permit estimating the coefficient of variable maintenance costs on other than paved surfaces. Experience from other countries can, however, be used to indicate their relative magnitude.

The problem of determining the relationship between traffic volume and standard maintenance costs can be solved mainly by the development of experimental data and the collection of statistical material on a wider basis than is possible in Central America. From this basic data it should be possible to estimate the variable maintenance costs of trucks, cars, etc. on different types of road surfaces. This need only be done in one country and the results modified for application in other climates. In addition to providing guidelines for establishing user charges, such results could be used to control maintenance expenditures and to allocate spending more efficiently. In the absence of such guidelines, policy recommendations must be appropriately qualified and tentative. It will be apparent from Chapter VIII that the conclusions and recommendations of this study in relation to road user charges are presented in a way that reflects the uncertain empirical knowledge of maintenance costs.

Investment and Location

Investment in roads is one of the most important types of decisions made by the road authorities. In Chapter II, it was shown that the solutions of efficient prices (EUC's) and the efficient investment program are interdependent. The main problem is that price and revenue do not provide any simple signal to indicate the desirability of investment programs. Choice between alternative projects should be based on an analysis of benefits, only part of which may be recovered in the form of revenue for the road authority. Cost-benefit studies provide the appropriate criteria for decision on investment allocation. Even when the prices or user charges are fixed at levels other than the EUC, one can use cost-benefit analysis to find the second best investment policy; this then gives the appropriate rules for investment given that the user charges are fixed at certain specified values.

This is clearly the approach to be used in evaluating the investment programs of Central America. The user charges levied in 1967 were the result of historical accidents. But, taking these charges as given, one can investigate the investment policy that has been pursued in the past and the pattern of location that has been generated. It is beyond the scope of this study to investigate the detailed investment criteria that were used, but in practice it is not difficult

---

[15] This may largely be a function of road design. The AASHO Road Test results indicate that on a road designed for heavy vehicles that damage (loss of serviceability) varies little with vehicle weight for axle loads and tire sizes within appropriate limits but may increase sharply if these limits are exceeded.

to identify the most glaring inadequacies in the road system, and to make broad judgments about the desirability of projects both ex post and ex ante.

The following section will be devoted to (i) analyzing some institutional aspects of road investment decisions in the Central American countries and evaluating in general terms past road investment decisions, and (ii) investigating the pattern of location of industry and agriculture and its relationship to road investment (and road pricing).

Road investment policy in Central America

Road investment in paved and all-weather roads has in the past been concentrated on the Pacific slopes of the Central American isthmus, while the Atlantic coast still only accounts for a relatively small fraction of the total road network. Road investment in the past 15 years has concentrated on connecting in each country the major centers of consumption and production (the capitals) with the ports and, for the region as a whole, in providing the links between the capitals of all the Central American countries (the Pan-American Highway). With the exception of Honduras, the Pan-American Highway still forms the backbone of the road system in each country. The bulk of past road investment was thus aimed at providing the most important and obvious connections, while only in recent years has more emphasis been given to extending the road network to open up new agricultural land (feeder roads, farm to market roads, etc.). For reasons which are discussed in more detail in Chapter VII, road investment in the cities has lagged substantially behind that in the rest of the country.

As external lending has accounted for a substantial part of total road financing (except in Nicaragua) investment decisions in roads were arrived at in close cooperation with external lending agencies.[16] External lending took place either directly via the international and bilateral lending agencies or indirectly, via the Central American Bank for Integration (CABEI), which in turn is mainly financed through United States A.I.D. resources.

Superficially judging past road investment decisions on the basis of traffic count and applying the very crude rule of thumb that certain traffic volumes justify certain types of road improvements, the conclusion can be reached that past interurban and rural road investment in Central America was by and large well justified. This in itself is probably not surprising since most of the roads built or improved appear to be "obvious" cases (major through connec-

---

[16] For the five countries external funds accounted for 44 percent of total construction expenditures between 1960–65 (57 percent in Guatemala, 40 percent in El Salvador, 62 percent in Honduras, 21 percent in Nicaragua and 44 percent in Costa Rica). See IBRD *Economic Development and Prospects of Central America*, Vol. VI, p. 4.

tions, etc.) where high rates of return are to be expected. But while inter-urban and rural road development has in some degree kept pace with need, road investment in the cities in all the Central American countries seems to have been badly neglected. If the same criteria used for rural roads are applied to urban streets, it is obvious that very high rates of return are associated with urban investment. Because these investments were neglected, vehicle operating costs and congestion costs (private and social) in the cities have increased rapidly in recent years. The reasons for this lack of emphasis on urban investment are mainly the lack of funds and inefficient city administration. Cities have not had an adequate revenue base and external lending agencies have not been interested in financing urban road projects.

The larger part of the externally financed projects were justified in terms of savings in operating costs of existing traffic; benefits from future traffic growth only played a secondary role in the justification of these projects.[17] This trend will probably be reversed in the future, since a substantial part of the major through connections are built or are being built. More emphasis will have to be given to opening up new agricultural areas through the construction of feeder and penetration roads. Investment decisions will become more difficult the less reliance can be placed on simple user cost savings estimates. Hence improving the information needed to make sound investment decisions becomes very important.

There is in Central America substantial scope for improving data collection at relatively moderate costs. A useful way of providing some of this information would be to undertake investment reappraisal studies on a more regular basis. This could be done on a far simpler and less costly basis than for instance that used in the Iran Study.[18] The systematic collection of data on freight rates before and after improvement of roads, and agricultural production figures along improved or newly constructed roads, could already substantially enlarge and improve the basis on which future investment decisions are made.[19]

---

[17] See IBRD Appraisal Reports: G 124; HO 195; HO 400; HO 495; CR 299; ES 216/521.

[18] See H. G. van der Tak and J. de Weille, *Reappraisal of a Road Project in Iran,* World Bank Staff Occasional Paper No. 7 (Baltimore: The Johns Hopkins Press, 1969).

[19] Freight rates appear to be a very useful check for the standard operating cost savings coefficients (mostly originating in the same US source) which are used in most appraisal reports. The change (or lack of change) in freight rates when transport costs are lowered serves as a good indicator of the competitive situation in the transport industry. In El Salvador, for example, the mission observed that bus fares had not changed in the last decade, although transport costs over most of the system had fallen. Since passenger transport is heavily regulated in El Salvador, this is not surprising.

In Chapter VI of this study an attempt is made to analyze the impact of highway investment on agricultural production. The model developed here can be usefully extended to cover a number of situations typically found and could serve as the basis for investment decisions in the type of road investment that will be of increasing importance in Central America. This work could be undertaken by both national road authorities and by international agencies, and might aid such agencies as the Central American Bank for Economic Integration (CABEI) in making difficult regional (as opposed to national) investments.[20]

Road investment and location of industrial and agricultural activity in Central America

From what has been said thus far about the pattern of past road investment in the Central American countries, the locational pattern of economic activities can already be conjectured.

Industrial activities today are either centered around the major ports (if imported raw materials are very bulky) or the major markets which are identical with the capitals of each country (except for San Pedro Sula, Honduras). Road investment was probably not the leading location factor, but rather followed the other overriding location factors such as markets and supply of raw materials. Location of industrial activity within the Common Market appears to have been very little influenced by investments in regional roads (Pan-American Highway, Littoral); other factors were instrumental in distributing industrial activities between the Central American countries. High border crossing costs and high transport costs in general protected most of the light industries, with the result that most countries today have the same type of light industrial activities.[21] For other industries where economies of scale are more important the competitive granting of tax exemptions appears to have been the most important location factor.[22] All of the countries have made great efforts in the past to attract new industries by granting tax exemptions.

---

[20] Regional road projects, i.e. basically roads which are to link the national road systems into a regional system, are to a large extent financed by CABEI. The member countries of the Common Market have agreed on a list of regional roads (Central American roads). The regional status of a road appears to be based not solely on economic but on political grounds as well. Hence the danger of uneconomic road investment decisions as a result of political quid pro quo should not be overlooked—especially as CABEI loans are made at very favorable terms.

[21] Of course it is conceivable that in the light industries operated in Central America economies of scale are not important.

[22] For a more detailed discussion of this issue, see IBRD *Economic Development and Prospects in Central America*, Main Report, p. 38.

The location of agricultural production on the other hand, appears to have been closely related to the availability of road transport. The map on p. 60 presents some evidence to this effect. The highest growth rates of agricultural land utilization between 1952 and 1963 are found mainly in those areas where road construction or improvement has taken place. Most road construction was designed to provide through connections between major production and consumption areas and ports, and agricultural development took place along these major arteries.

Road investments (complemented with the appropriate pricing policy) are likely to play an important role in the location of economic activities in the future. In the industrial sector the Common Market partners are at present working toward discontinuing the indiscriminate and competitive granting of tax exemptions. They are also investigating the problem of excessive border crossing costs. If these were eliminated transport costs would become a more important factor in locating industrial activities, particularly for those products with high bulk and low value where transport costs account for a large fraction of the final price. Location of agricultural production will probably continue to be heavily influenced by the availability of road services. Most of the incremental agricultural production is likely to be located in areas yet to be penetrated or in extensions of existing areas. Feeder roads and penetration roads will play an important role.

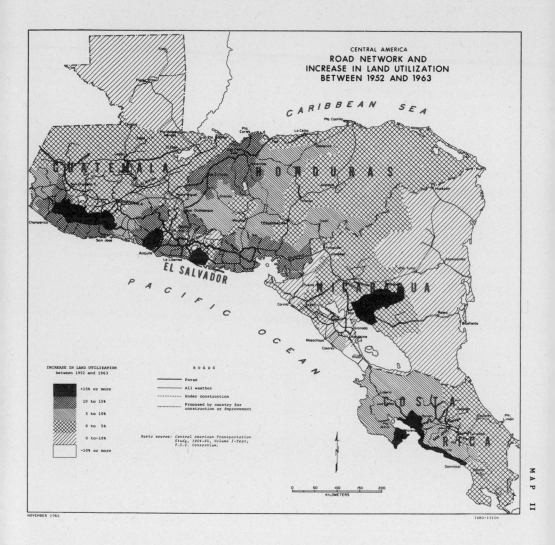

CENTRAL AMERICA
ROAD NETWORK AND
INCREASE IN LAND UTILIZATION
BETWEEN 1952 AND 1963

CARIBBEAN SEA

GUATEMALA

HONDURAS

EL SALVADOR

PACIFIC OCEAN

NICARAGUA

COSTA RICA

INCREASE IN LAND UTILIZATION
between 1952 and 1963

+15% or more
10 to 15%
5 to 10%
0 to 5%
0 to -10%
-10% or more

ROADS

———— Paved
———— All weather
---------- Under construction
············ Proposed by country for
construction or improvement

*Basic source: Central American Transportation
Study, 1964-65, Volume I-Text;
T.S.C. Consortium.*

0   50   100   150   200
KILOMETERS

MAP II

V

PRESENT ROAD TAXES AND CHARGES

Introduction

The terms user charge and user tax are used synonymously in this study.[1] The choice of a definition was based on its usefulness in analyzing a system of user charges. In order to be workable the definition must make it possible to include (or exclude) with ease and clarity any item from the user charge category. The following scheme has these characteristics. First, if a good or service used in transportation (other than the services of the road) is sold to the user at a price equal to its "opportunity costs" no user charge exists. Second, if this good or service is sold at a price above its "opportunity cost," and if this difference between price and cost is caused by government action (for instance the creation of a government monopoly to manufacture tires), whether or not such action results in additional overt government revenues, then a user charge has been levied. The user charge is thus the difference between price of the good or service and its "opportunity cost."

Opportunity cost is defined as the lowest cost of the good or service in terms of the value of the resource required to produce it—assuming that government policy imposes no impediments. Thus, for example:

---

[1] This is done because it appears to be common practice. It would be preferable to be more precise as to the meaning of these terms.

a) The opportunity cost of a tire in the Central American market is its import cost. This is true in spite of the fact that tires are produced domestically at high cost. The alternative that would in fact (at least currently) be resorted to would be the international market. Hence, in accordance with the definition, the tire tax is the difference between local price and import price.

b) The crossing of international borders in Central America involves a cost of US\$40 to US\$60 per truck. The cheapest alternative not consistent with other major objectives, is to drive the truck over the line with no expenditure of resources. The user charge then consists of the entire US\$40 to US\$60.

This definition is, however, insufficient for purposes of analysis. It is necessary to go one step further in order to equate costs and prices. In order to do this it is necessary to define a new term, net user charges, which is the user charge as defined above minus the cost of the resources wasted as a result of a specified government policy.[2] In terms of the examples above, the net user charge becomes:

a) The domestic production of tires, fixed in the short-run by capacity limits, falls short of consumption in Central America. Therefore at the margin imported tires are purchased, and the net user charge is the difference between the domestic price and the international price. (If on the other hand the imports were restricted by quota and domestic industry expanded its output to meet increases in domestic consumption, the net user charge would be zero or close to it.)

b) In the case of the border crossing the subtraction of the resources wasted as a result of government policy would yield a net user charge of zero, since the user charge is equal to the resources consumed.

In this chapter only the net user charges are considered. The difference between the net user charge and what might be called the "gross" user charge is discussed in Chapter III under the heading of Quasi-tax Elements of Transport Cost.

Road taxation in Central America

The following sections discuss in some detail the various taxes levied on road users in Central America. In order to place the discussion of the individual taxes within a broader framework, Table 5.1 summarizes the taxes levied per vehicle kilometer for several classes of vehicles on paved roads.

---

[2] It should be obvious here that the definition is in terms of marginal costs.

TABLE 5.1: Total Taxes on Road Users on Paved Roads

(US cents per veh/km)

	Guatemala	El Salvador	Honduras	Nicaragua	Costa Rica
Passenger Car					
Fuel taxes	.47	.54	.42	.36	.47
Tire taxes	.04	.04	.03	.04	.06
Purchase taxes	.96	.96	.26	.88	1.87
Sales taxes	.17	–	.40	–	1.41
License fees	.20	.11	.44	.22	.16
Total	1.84	1.65	1.55	1.50	3.97
7-Ton Truck (Gasoline)					
Fuel taxes	1.72	1.99	1.54	1.32	1.72
Tire taxes	.15	.15	.12	.15	.18
Purchase taxes	.28	.31	–	.56	.77
Sales taxes	–	–	–	–	–
License fees	.29	.19	–	.07	.09
Total	2.44	2.64	1.66	2.10	2.76
18-Ton Truck (Diesel)					
Fuel taxes	.36	.18	.24	.23	0
Tire taxes	.37	.38	.29	.38	.43
Purchase taxes	.31	.34	–	.61	.79
Sales taxes	–	–	–	–	–
License fees	.24	.48	0	.04	.09
Total	1.28	1.38	.53	1.26	1.31

Source: Table 5.9.

Although the incidence of the absolute level of taxes differs from country to country for different vehicle categories, the structure of road taxes for a given type of vehicle is quite similar in all Central American countries.[3] Taxes on fuel form the basis of taxation for most vehicle types, with vehicle purchases taxes being important for passenger cars and heavy trucks. Tire taxes are only important for the heavier, more tire intensive vehicles.

License duties vary substantially from country to country. Some idea of this variation can be seen by assuming that all vehicles do the same amount of traveling on the same type of road surface (paved). The figures were obtained by dividing annual license fees by average vehicle kilometers traveled for the various types of vehicles.

---

[3] The only cases clearly out of line are passenger cars in Costa Rica, which pay more than double per veh/km than in the next highest country, and heavy diesel trucks in Honduras which are charged only about one half of what is charged in other countries.

The crucial factor here is, of course, the assumption made regarding annual kilometers. In estimating the incidence of purchase taxes a similar assumption had to be made with respect to vehicle service life. In both cases for lack of any other information the data provided by the de Weille Study were used.[4] Some evidence from other countries at a similar stage of development suggests that the de Weille figures may be high both with respect to annual kilometers and vehicle service life. Reducing annual kilometers by one-third increases the incidence of the license fee on vehicle kilometers by nearly 50 percent in the case of the seven-ton truck. A shorter vehicle service life similarly increases the incidence of purchase taxes. The net effect of changing these two assumptions is that it increases total user charges by approximately 20 to 25 percent for the larger trucks in all countries except Honduras.[5]

In the case of the fuel tax, the assumption made about vehicle mileage per gallon of fuel is taken from de Weille and is shown in the footnote to Table 5.9. This evidently overstates miles per gallon of gasoline (see the estimates in the table on page 84) by about 100 percent. Since this is the most important tax, present user charges per mile may be very much higher than the estimates given here. Thus the economic importance of the overcharges discussed in the next chapter is probably greater than estimated.

Fuel Taxes[6]

Taxes on fuels are of major importance in most systems of road taxes. These taxes have the advantage of being easy to collect and enforce but have the disadvantage of bearing little relationship to the costs of using the road. In addition because of their direct impact upon the cost of transport they may, when being used as a source of revenue, result in under-utilization (or conversely excess queuing when roads are crowded) of capacity. Fuel taxes are generally applied in their most simple form, i.e., as a specific levy (cents per US gallon). The same flat rate generally applies to different fuel qualities, although in many cases the tax rate is varied between diesel and gasoline fuel. In one country (Nicaragua) the tax rate even differentiates between regular and extra gasoline.

---

[4] Jan de Weille, *Quantification of Road User Savings*, World Bank Staff Occasional Paper No. 2 (Baltimore: The Johns Hopkins Press, 1966).

[5] This is relevant to the discussion in Chapter VI where the consequences of having prices in excess of costs are considered.

[6] In addition to fuel taxes, import duties on lubricants are levied in Central America. Since they are only of minor importance both from the point of view of revenues collected as well as their incidence per veh/km they are not further discussed in this study. (For rates see Table 5.7.)

TABLE 5.2: Fuel Taxes in Central America

	Guatemala	El Salvador	Honduras	Nicaragua	Costa Rica
Tax Rate (*cents per gallon*)					
Gasoline	22.2	25.6	19.8	17.0	22.3
Diesel	5.3	2.6	3.5	3.3	0
Tax Incidence, (paved roads) (*cents per veh/km*)					
Passenger car (gasoline)	.5	.5	.4	.4	.5
7-ton truck (gasoline)	1.7	2.0	1.5	1.3	1.7
18-ton truck (diesel)	.4	.2	.2	.2	0
Revenues Collected, 1966					
Mill. US$	10.0	6.6	2.1	2.7	6.2
As % of total road tax revenues	57		58	45	61

Source: Tables 5.6 and 3.9.

Table 5.2 summarizes the present system of fuel taxes in five Central American countries in terms of tax rates, tax incidence per vehicle kilometer for different vehicle categories and revenues collected.

The Central American fuel tax system is characterized by large rate differentials between gasoline and diesel fuel. The differential is least in Guatemala, where diesel fuel pays less than one-fourth as much per gallon as gasoline; in Costa Rica there is no tax at all on diesel fuel. This is in the face of generally higher consumption per ton/km of diesel fuel than of gasoline. Gasoline is very heavily taxed, not only in absolute terms but also relative to the level of fuel taxes in other countries in the Hemisphere.[7] Fuel taxes are clearly the single most important revenue source among road taxes—accounting for between 60 to 70 percent of total revenues collected from road duties in different countries.

Fuel taxes and variable road maintenance costs

Fuel consumption per ton kilometer varies with the type of fuel, the size and power of vehicle, the type of road surface, traffic conditions and the degree of horizontal and vertical curvature. The differences are substantial, making it difficult to use fuel taxes to approximate costs of road services not only for a given type of road surface (where variations are the result of speed, vehicle type and curvature), but particularly between types of road surfaces which

---

[7] For example: U.S. 11.25 cents per gallon; Argentina: 10.3 cents per gallon; Brazil: 25.1 cents per gallon; Chile: 10.1 cents per gallon; Colombia: 1.7 cents per gallon; Mexico: 6.2 cents per gallon; Peru: 4.2 cents per gallon.

can result in great differences in fuel consumption.[8] A passenger car, for example, will consume gasoline in a ratio of 1 :1.2 :1.4 over paved-gravel-dirt roads, whereas the estimated variable maintenance cost of using these roads varies in a ratio of 1 :11 :33. Thus it is not possible to design a fuel tax that will adequately reflect these cost ratios. This may be further illustrated by looking at how present fuel tax rates approximate the cost of using roads with different surfaces. The incidence of fuel taxes per vehicle/km for a passenger car in Guatemala amounts to .5 cents on paved, .6 cents on gravel and .7 cents on earth roads, against variable road maintenance costs of .1, 1.1 and 3.3 cents per veh/km.[9] The best that can be done is to design the fuel tax to approximate the costs on one type of road surface of a given design (i.e., an average road section) and assume that vehicles are of an "average" type and travel at "average" speeds. This is not as unrealistic as it would first appear; while speed and curvature result in different rates of fuel consumption, the largest differences by far are accounted for by the type of road surface, and as was found in Central America, the majority of veh/km travelled (over 70 percent) were on one type of road surface.[10] If fuel taxes were to be used exclusively to approximate variable road maintenance costs on paved roads, present tax rates for gasoline would have to be substantially reduced, since at present rates gasoline-using vehicles are overcharged from 4 to 20 times. (See Table 5.1.) Present tax rates for diesel fuel come much closer to reflecting the variable maintenance cost—VMC—(except in Costa Rica, where no diesel tax is levied). In Honduras and El Salvador the incidence of the diesel tax per vehicle/km is only about twice the estimated VMC.

Additional problems are introduced when there are variations in types and octane ratings of fuel, with the greatest variations occurring between the use of diesel and gasoline. These two types of fuels require engines with different operating characteristics and cost functions. Vehicles using either diesel or gasoline engines are to some extent substitutes for each other; therefore taxes imposed upon these fuels in order to approximate variable maintenance costs must not, if inefficiencies are to be avoided, distort the cost-price ratios. The following example will clarify this point. A seven-ton truck with a diesel engine will travel approximately 17 kilometers on a gallon (US gallon) of diesel fuel, while the same truck with a gasoline engine will run 13 kilometers on a gallon of gas.[11] If the economic user charge is one cent per kilometer a

---

[8] De Weille.

[9] For variable road maintenance cost data see Chapter IV.

[10] See Chapter III, Table 3.1.

[11] These figures were drawn from studies in the U.K. They may overstate the kilometers obtainable from both types of fuel in the Central American region where trucks are of a different design and the terrain generally mountainous.

gallon of diesel fuel should bear a tax of 17 cents and a gallon of gas 13 cents. The higher efficiency of the diesel engine means that diesel fuel should be taxed at a higher rate than gasoline, the converse of what is the traditional pattern of most countries. The tax applicable to diesel may be even higher if it is assumed that it is used exclusively by heavy vehicles which cause greater damage to the road than the lighter gasoline powered vehicles. Large rate differentials in the wrong direction between diesel and gasoline fuels are typical in Central America.

This tax differential is substantially larger than the relative costs of producing the two fuels, thereby encouraging an inefficient use of the two fuel categories. The point may be illustrated in the case of El Salvador: the ex-refinery price of locally refined fuel is 10.2 cents and 8.6 cents per gallon for regular gasoline and diesel respectively, or a ratio of prices of 1.19:1. Adding the tax (not taking into account for the moment distribution margins and transportation costs) the prices increase to 35.9 for gasoline and 11.2 for diesel, or a price ratio of 2.2:1. Fuel consumption data available for El Salvador do in fact indicate that the large tax differential has lead to a spectacular increase in diesel consumption (33 percent per annum between 1960–66) against a comparatively modest increase for gasoline (5.6 percent per annum in the same period). At present data are not available to make a quantitative judgment regarding the inefficiencies in fuel and vehicle use resulting from the discrimination against gasoline fuel. One would have to know how total transport costs of the two vehicle categories are influenced by the differential tax incidence. Generally, diesel engines use less fuel than comparable gasoline engines but are more expensive to purchase and maintain, although service lives tend to be longer. Note that in Costa Rica, where no diesel tax has been levied in recent years, diesel powered vehicles have by far outnumbered gasoline vehicles in the heavy truck category.[12]

In principle a similar efficiency problem is raised in the taxation of fuels of different octane grades. Higher octane ratings usually increase the distance which can be travelled per gallon, and thus if the cost of using the road is a specified amount per kilometer the tax per gallon on higher octane fuels should be higher than for regular grades. Again this can be illustrated with present road taxes in Central America. In all Central American countries (except in Nicaragua) a simple specific tax is charged to all gasoline regardless of octane rating. The cost differentials between the fuel grades presently refined in Central America (they do not exceed 93–95 octanes) are, however, rather small. In the case of El Salvador, for example, the ex-refinery prices amount to 10.2 cents and 12.1 cents for regular and extra gasoline respectively. Adding the

---

[12] See Chapter III, p. 28.

67

tax of 25.7 cents in both cases, the resulting price is 35.9 cents and 37.8 cents (excluding distribution margins and transportation costs). The ratio between the production costs is 1:1.18 while the ratio between production costs plus taxes is reduced to 1:1.05. Hence the discrimination against vans and trucks using regular gasoline and in favor of cars using high octane gasoline seems less important than in the gasoline-diesel case. Nevertheless, in recent years consumption of the higher cost premium gasoline increased substantially faster than that of regular.[13]

Fuel taxes and congestion costs

The practical possibilities of using differential fuel taxes to reflect congestion costs appear to be rather limited although the principle is clear. One may conceivably differentiate fuel taxes either between different locations or between different categories of vehicles.

In the former case one would charge higher fuel tax rates in the cities and lower rates in the rest of the country. Given the large difference between variable road maintenance costs on non-congested interurban roads and the cost of congestion on urban streets (the latter being up to 60 times as much as the former) the tax differential would have to be so large that it would invite fuel carrying journeys which would almost be impossible to police. Hence the limits of a differential fuel tax set by the cost of transporting fuel. Nevertheless, within these limits the differential fuel tax should still be considered as a (small) part of a congestion tax package.[14] In this sense it is of interest to notice that the fuel price structure in some of the Central American countries (and for that matter probably in most developing countries) works in the opposite direction. Fuel prices are generally at a minimum close to the refinery or port of entry—which in many countries is close to the major urban centers —and are generally higher in rural areas due to the increased transport costs. In Honduras, for example, the spread between the highest and the lowest fuel prices amounts to 7.5 cents for gasoline and 10.0 cents for diesel, or almost

---

[13] It increased at a rate of 46 percent per annum between 1960–65 as against 5.5 percent for regular. However, it has to be noted that premium gasoline started from a very low level (6 percent of total gasoline consumption in 1960), but nevertheless by 1966 had increased its share to 40 percent of total consumption.

[14] The difficulties of administering fuel taxes on the local level (collection at the pumphead rather than at the refinery or import level) do not seem to be insuperable in practice. In Guatemala a municipal gasoline tax (2 cents per gallon) is already in force, the collection of which—at least for Guatemala City (60 percent of the country's fuel consumption)—is based on sales to individual gas stations.

68

⅓ of the gasoline tax and three times the diesel tax. Except for the fuel prices charged along the south coast (from where fuel is mainly imported), the prices in Tegucigalpa, the chief urban center, are the lowest in the country (almost 5 cents below the prices charged in the rest of the country both for diesel and gasoline). This suggests that it might be at least worthwhile to consider a differential fuel tax which would offset the present "perverse" (from a congestion point of view) price structure. A second possibility of fuel tax differentiation exists by utilizing the fuel differences of some types of vehicles. If, for instance, diesel powered vehicles used the intercity and rural highway network and gasoline powered vehicles urban streets, then it would be possible to consider a differential diesel/gasoline tax as an instrument to charge for congestion costs. The veh/km travelled by vehicles in the two categories do not, however, appear to be so neatly separated in Central America. Although some observations (see page 115) confirm that trucks mainly use non-urban roads and passenger cars urban streets, only about 11 percent of total trucks in Guatemala for instance have diesel engines.[15] Hence by having high gasoline taxes (reflecting congestion costs of passenger cars with gasoline engines using city streets) one would, at least in some countries, overcharge a large fraction of total truck veh/km whose incidence is not predominately on city streets.

Fuel taxes and raising revenues

The above paragraphs have considered only the role of the fuel tax in approximating the EUC. There remains to be examined its role in raising government revenues. Here each case must be examined separately. There is no doubt that substantial revenues can (and in most countries are) raised by means of fuel taxes, but this in itself cannot be regarded as the sole end of public policy. The effect of the tax upon the distribution of resources must be considered. Like almost any tax, a tax on fuel will discourage the use of the good taxed. (Tax is used here in the sense of a charge over and above that necessary to cover the variable maintenance or congestion costs.) In the case of the fuel tax, the incidence will differ widely depending upon the type of good transported. The derived demand for the transport of heavy, low-value items usually has a high elasticity.[16] A fuel tax will thus tend to discourage the movement of such goods.

---

[15] See Chapter III, p. 28. The distribution between diesel and gasoline trucks is however different in Costa Rica, where about 75% of heavy trucks have diesel engines. No data are available for other countries.

[16] The elasticity of demand for transport is proportional to the ratio of the transport cost to the c.i.f. price. The factor of proportionality depends on the demand and supply elasticities.

In addition these taxes will change the transport production function. The same tax on diesel oil and gasoline (or regular and super gasoline), whether specific or ad valorem, will change the consumption pattern of these fuels as the tax is not likely to bear any relationship to their relative engineering or economic efficiencies. Fuel taxes can thus lead to a variety of distorting effects. In addition to those already discussed above high fuel taxes encourage the use of vehicles with a low power/weight ratio using less fuel per ton transported. This would increase congestion since vehicles with low power/weight ratios give rise to more congestion than vehicles with higher power/weight ratios. High fuel taxes could also tend to lead to a substitution of rail for road transport not justified by relative efficiencies.

Administration and exemptions

Fuel taxes, with one minor exception in Guatemala, are always specific and levied either in the form of production taxes in countries having their own refineries (Guatemala, El Salvador, Nicaragua and Costa Rica) or in the form of an import duty in countries relying on imported fuels (Costa Rica and Honduras). The administration of fuel taxes is relatively simple in that they are levied at the refinery or import level according to sales to the distributors. In Honduras the import duty collection is based on the changes in the inventories of the distributor firms at the ports of Puerto Cortes and Cutuco (El Salvador). In the very near future, however, Honduras will also have its own refinery in operation so that the import duty will be replaced by a domestic production tax. Domestic refineries are protected by additional duties (5 cents per gallon in Guatemala and 7 cents in El Salvador)[17] over and above the internal taxes. Except for the fuel types not locally produced, no imports take place. Most of the refineries work substantially below their capacities.

The government (including municipalities and autonomous agencies), the diplomatic corps and the railways are exempt from fuel taxes in all countries. Data available for Guatemala indicate that these exemptions affect quite a substantial part of total consumption. In 1965 the exemptions amounted to 1.9 million dollars or ⅓ of revenues collected. In addition to the above mentioned exemptions Honduras also exempts agricultural machines, tractors, etc. from paying fuel taxes. Except in the case of agricultural machinery and the railways these exemptions have absolutely no relation to the cost of using the roads. From the point of view of efficient administration and of a rational decision-making for road use it would be preferable if the government would also be charged road taxes.

---

[17] At present, no system of taxes has been established for the future refining operation in Honduras.

70

Tire Taxes[18]

Because tire wear varies with the use of the road, a tax on tires can be regarded as direct user charge. The most simple form of a tire tax would be a specific tax (i.e., x cents per kg of rubber) either levied as a production or an import duty. Administratively somewhat more complicated because of the need to assess values would be an ad valorem tire tax.

In Central America a mixture of ad valorem plus specific import duties are levied on tires. Table 5.3 summarizes rates, incidence per veh/km and revenue collection of present tire taxes:

TABLE 5.3: Tire Taxes in Central America

	Common Tariff				
	Guate-mala	El Salvador	Nicaragua	Costa Rica	Honduras
Rates (% and US$ per 100 kg)					
Produced in C.A.		10% + $90		a	$10
Not produced in C.A.		10% + $10		a	
Tax Incidence (US cents per veh/km)					
Passenger car	.04	.04	.04	.05	.03
7-ton truck	.2	.2	.2	.2	.1
18-ton truck	.4	.4	.4	.4	.3
Revenues Collected in 1966					
Million US$	n.a.	n.a.	.9	.2	n.a.
% of total road taxes collected			15	3	

Source: Tables 5.9 and 3.9.
a In addition to import duties a consumption tax of US$4–7 for passenger car tires and of US$5–9 for truck tires is levied.

Only about half of total tire consumption in Central America is imported from countries outside the Central American Common Market. The other half is produced domestically by a firm in Guatemala[19] and no duties or sales taxes are levied (except in Honduras which did not join the agreement setting up a regional tire industry). Costa Rica has an internal excise tax of $5–9 for truck tires and $4–7 for passenger car tires. The protection granted in the Common Tariff to domestically produced tires varies for typical sizes from 49–51 percent of the value for passenger car tires and from 42–60 percent for truck tires. For tire sizes not produced in Guatemala the import duty amounts to 15 percent. The Honduran import duties on tires, expressed as an ad valorem rate, are lower and amount to about 33 percent for passenger car

---

[18] See also the discussion of the tire industry, Chapter III.
[19] By the end of 1968 a new firm in Costa Rica should start to account for a significant percentage of the market.

71

tires and between 32 and 42 percent for truck tires. Correspondingly, the tax element in market prices amounts to between 28 and 40 percent for truck tires (34 percent for passenger car tires) in the countries applying the common tariff and between 24 and 30 percent for truck tires (25 percent for passenger car tires) in Honduras.

In spite of these substantial tax rates, revenues collected from tire taxes are very low. In 1966 they amounted to about $.2 million ($.9 million) or 3 percent (15%) of total road taxes collected in Costa Rica (Nicaragua).

Tire taxes and variable maintenance costs

Of all the ton/kilometer or vehicle taxes, tire taxes come closest to measuring the relative variable maintenance costs of different road surfaces. The ratio of tire wear between paved, gravel and earth roads amounts to about 1:2:3.5 for cars and 1:2:4.5 for trucks[20] while the corresponding variation of variable road maintenance costs amounts to 1:11:33.[21] Hence even a tire tax is far from perfect and in general can reflect the cost ratios only very crudely. Nevertheless, in the case of heavy (tire intensive) trucks the present tax rates levied in Central America (Common Tariff) approximate VMC's much better than the above ratios suggested. The tire tax incidence for an 18-ton truck per vehicle kilometer varies between .4 cents for paved, 1.5 cents for gravel and 3.7 cents for earth roads compared to the estimated VMC's of .1, 1.1 and 3.3 cents respectively.[22] The approximation of VMC's, however, is substantially less accurate for lighter vehicles. If tire taxes were to be used exclusively to reflect VMC's on paved roads, then present tax rates would have to be somewhat increased for passenger cars and reduced (except in Honduras) for trucks.

Tire taxes and congestion costs

There is no opportunity for employing the tire tax to reflect congestion costs. It is impossible to distinguish administratively between the use of tires in congested and rural situations. One might suggest that since most congestion is caused by private cars it would be useful to levy high taxes on those tires used on such cars. Such a differentiation would be a very rough and ready recognition of congestion since probably about half the private car mileage experiences uncongested conditions.

---

[20] De Weille, p. 64.

[21] See Chapter IV.

[22] Assuming (for the present) that heavy vehicles and light vehicles cause the same amount of damage per kilometer.

72

Tire taxes and revenue raising

Tires do not provide a good basis for levying taxes for general revenue purposes (as opposed to their use for approximating the *EUC*). This is because annual expenditure on tires accounts for only a small proportion of transport costs. In addition, because of their size, excessively high taxes encourage a contraband trade (see page 71). The effects on safety, although they cannot be quantified with present data, are clearly not insignificant. High tire taxes may contribute to accidents.[23] The low annual expenditures on tires and the tax exemption of about half of total consumption in Central America contributes to the relatively modest revenues collected despite the high tax rates.

Vehicle Purchase Taxes

For analytical purposes it is simpler to consider together both import duties and domestic sales taxes on vehicles. Differences occur only when there is a domestic industry competing with imports, and consideration of this case is more properly left to a discussion of general transport and import policy.

Vehicle purchase taxes (both import and domestic taxes) are levied on new or newly imported cars only. This distinguishes them from license duties which are charged to both new and old vehicles in the form of an annual fee. Vehicle purchase taxes increase the price of the product to be depreciated, and to the extent that depreciation is a result of use and not merely passage of time, they increase the cost to the user of increased mileage. To that extent they fall on vehicle operating cost and hence can be considered a charge to use the road system. License fees, on the other hand, are not closely related to the use of vehicles.[24]

Vehicle purchase taxes are levied in a wide variety of forms depending on the goals that are to be achieved (raising revenues, discouraging certain forms of consumption, etc.). The most common forms are either a straight ad valorem tax (percent of declared value), a progressive ad valorem or a specific levy (varied according to weight, horsepower, etc.). See below, Table 5.4.

Except for Honduras the progressive rates of vehicle purchase taxes for passenger cars (combining import duties and sales taxes) are clearly designed to discourage luxury consumption. Trucks and buses, on the other hand, are only very lightly taxed. Revenues collected from purchase taxes are quite sub-

---

[23] It would be possible to counter this effect by paying rebates based on the weight of old tires.

[24] Purchase of a license gives one the right to use the vehicle on the public highway, but the license duty does not vary with the number of miles covered.

TABLE 5.4:   Vehicle Purchase Taxes in Central America

	Guate-mala	El Salvador	Honduras	Nicaragua	Costa Rica
Rates (*% and US$ per 100 kg*)					
Passenger cars	55	40	15	40	50% + $79–127
Under $2,000	130	100		70	
Over $4,000	10	11	0	20	22% + $3
Trucks					
Tax Incidence, Paved Roads (*US cents per veh/km*)					
Passenger cars	1.1	1.0	.9	.9	1.9
7-ton trucks	.3	.3	nil	.6	.8
18-ton trucks	.3	.3	nil	.6	.8
Revenues Collected 1966					
Million US$	4.5	3.6	.9	1.6	2.3
% of total road taxes collected	26	30	25	27	23

Source: Tables 5.9 and 3.8.

stantial. In terms of their contribution to total road taxes they rank second behind fuel taxes.

Vehicle purchase taxes and variable maintenance costs

Since the cost of depreciation per veh/km increases from paved to gravel to earth roads, a tax falling on depreciation can in principle be used to reflect the variable maintenance costs of roads. The rate of depreciation does not, however, vary in the same proportion as do variable maintenance costs. The variation of depreciation costs between different road surfaces (1:1:1.8 for cars and 1:1.5:2.5 for trucks on paved, gravel and earth roads respectively) approximate variable maintenance costs for different road surfaces to a lesser degree than tire wear.[25] With present tax rates in Guatemala the incidence per veh/km of purchase taxes for a passenger car would amount to 1.1 cents on paved, 1.4 cents on gravel and 2.0 cents on earth roads compared to variable road maintenance costs of .1 cents, 1.1 cents and 3.3 cents per vehicle kilometer.[26] With substantially lower tax rates for trucks the incidence per veh/km for a 7-ton truck would vary from .3 cents to .5 cents and .8 cents between paved, gravel and earth roads respectively.

In order to approximate the VMC a specific tax related to vehicle characteristic is called for. The tax should vary according to the road costs generated by the vehicle characteristics; heavy trucks should, for example, be taxed at higher rates than light vehicles if the former cause more damage to the road

[25] De Weille, p. 22.
[26] See Chapter IV, pp. 50–51.

than the latter. The present rate structure of vehicle purchase taxes in all the Central American countries is working in the opposite direction, however.

Vehicle purchase taxes and congestion charges

The appropriateness of vehicle purchase taxes for reflecting congestion costs depends largely on the possibility of distinguishing between vehicles which exclusively or predominantly use either congested or uncongested roads and the possibilities of substitution. Given the large duty differential between trucks, buses and passenger cars in Central America, the question arises whether the heavier incidence of this tax falls on those vehicles which are exclusively or at least predominantly responsible for the congestion in the cities. Earlier in this chapter it was pointed out that in Central America trucks predominantly used intercity and rural roads and passenger cars, the urban road network—hence the present system would be working in the right direction. This would not be true for buses, however, since they appear to be important contributors to city street congestion.[27] It has to be emphasized that even if the assumptions regarding the incidence of vehicle kilometers of the two vehicles categories were correct, that present rate would still be nowhere near the estimated congestion charge.[28]

It might be worthwhile to examine further the possibility of using vehicle taxes to reflect congestion costs in the case of Central America. The clear advantage of vehicle taxes, their direct impact on vehicle operating costs by affecting the costs of depreciation, is being (partly) offset by the difficulties of determining the vehicles which cause congestion and by the fact that there are possibilities of substitution. In addition, import duties or sales taxes have inequitable and distortive side effects. If duties or sales taxes are increased, the existing vehicle population receives a windfall gain. New vehicles are made more expensive and, as a result relatively fewer vehicles are imported or purchased and a relatively smaller stock of vehicles will carry the traffic.[29]

Vehicle purchase taxes and raising revenues

Import duties and sales taxes do have the advantage of being easy to administer and collect and thus are regarded as popular devices for raising public

---

[27] That is, bus fares do not reflect the cost of existing congestion. It is conceivable, however, that with appropriate charges for all vehicles more passengers might use the bus, thus causing bus congestion and in turn lower bus fares.

[28] The appropriate congestion charge for typical Central American conditions amounts to about 5 to 7 cents per vehicle/kilometer. The incidence of vehicle taxes for a passenger car in Guatemala is only 1.1 cent per vehicle/kilometer. See Chapter VII.

[29] Such a windfall gain could be compensated for by increasing license duties on old vehicles.

funds. When considered in this light they must be analyzed as any other tax and indeed should be regarded as part of the tax alternatives open to the government rather than as a tax specific to road use. It should not be forgotten, however, that the incidence of the tax will be in part on the use of the road system. Using these taxes as a way of approximating the EUC implies the application of a different criteria of taxation than if they were used as a source of general revenues. In the latter case one such criteria would be the ability to pay, that is, the taxation of luxury vehicles at higher rates. In addition to the raising of revenues, such taxes can be designed to discourage non-essential consumption. The use of these taxes for such purposes may conflict with their use as an approximation of the economic user charge. Any tax will have an effect upon the distribution of resources and the effects of these taxes (which happen to fall upon the use of roads) must be compared to the distorting effects of other taxes.

Additional problems may also be encountered when the tax is sufficiently high to change factor proportions. Taxes can change the consumption pattern of vehicles and, in the case where domestic production takes place, their design. The reaction of consumers to changes in relative prices through the imposition of a tax should always be taken into account when evaluating the impact of any tax.[30] This reaction will often offset some of the desirable aspects of the tax (raising revenues) by encouraging a wasteful use of resources. Progressive taxes based on the value of the vehicle can, for example, adversely affect the power/weight ratio of the vehicle, as this factor is often correlated with value. Such a tax changes the consumption pattern towards lighter and cheaper vehicles, which may prevent full utilization of the economies of scale inherent in larger vehicles or may encourage the uneconomic repair of vehicles. More intensive use of the existing stock of vehicles will be encouraged by high taxes.

License Fees and Tolls

A broad variety of license fees are possible and they may be designed so as to reflect numerous objectives such as approximating the variable maintenance costs, congestion costs, and raising revenues. Annual license fees usually have the impact of raising fixed annual costs and thus encouraging more intensive use of vehicles. On the other hand, restrictive licensing can have some impact on marginal costs or individual trip costs. The toll is an extreme example of such a restrictive "license" where a fee is extracted for the individual journey.

---

[30] The comments that follow are equally applicable to other taxes, particularly the fuel tax. High fuel taxes encourage the use of lighter, lower-powered vehicles. See also p. 65.

TABLE 5.5: Annual License Fees in Central America

(US$)

	Guatemala	El Salvador	Honduras	Nicaragua	Costa Rica
Rates					
Passenger car	30	16	75 (new) 50 (2 yrs old) 25 (5 or more)	33	20–30
Truck (7-ton)	158	100 (gas) 220 (diesel)	22 (new) 15 (2 yrs old) 7 (5 yrs old)	40	22
Tax Incidence, Paved Roads *(cents per veh/km)*					
Passenger car	.2	.1	.4	.2	.2
Trucks (7-ton)	.3	.4	.001	.07	.07
Revenues Collected 1966 Million US$	2.6	1.6	0.6	.5	1.3
% of total road taxes collected	15	14	17	12	13

Source: Tables 5.6 and 5.9.

The common form of license, however, is the non-restrictive one; this is usually an annual levy which once paid permits any degree of utilization of the road network. (See Table 5.5.)

Although the basis on which general license fees are levied can vary considerably there are broadly two types: those which are based on value and those which are based on capacity (capacity being defined in terms of weight or power). In Guatemala and El Salvador there are annual license fees on passenger vehicles that are simply flat rates, while in Honduras rates decrease with the age of the vehicle.[31] The level of license duties for passenger cars in Honduras is higher by quite a substantial margin than is the case in other countries. In the case of trucks the relative level of duties is substantially higher in Guatemala and El Salvador than in the rest of Central America. Honduras, Nicaragua and Costa Rica levy only nominal annual licenses while in Guatemala and El Salvador trucks are subject to fees which increase with weight. In addition, in El Salvador diesel trucks pay twice the rate of gasoline vehicles of the same weight.

License fees and variable maintenance costs

License fees are generally inappropriate as a method of approximating variable maintenance costs because the incidence of the tax is upon vehicle owner-

---

[31] There is also a municipal license fee in Honduras, $7.50 for cars and $12.50 for trucks.

TABLE 5.6: Road User Charges in Central America[a]

	Guatemala	El Salvador	Honduras	Nicaragua	Costa Rica
Gasoline Tax (*US cents per gal*)					
Central Government	19.6	25.6	19.8	17.0 (super 18.5)	22.3
Municipalities	2.0				
Sales tax	0.6				
Add. tax for imp. gasoline	5.0				
Diesel Oil Tax					
Sales tax (*% and US¢ per gal*)	5.0	2.58	3.45	3.3	0
Add. tax for imp. diesel	0.3				
(*US¢ per gal*)	5.0				
Lubricants, Oil (*% and US¢ per kg*)	10%	10% and 18¢	5¢		2% and 4¢
Import Duties (*% and US$ per 100 kg*)					
Passenger cars, all	–	40% (under 2.000)	15%		50% + $79
Up to 2,500	55%	50%			$127
2,500–3,000	55–80%	60%			
3,000–3,500	80–105%	70%			
3,500–4,000	105–130%	80%			
Over 4,000	130%	100%			
Buses	16%	11%	0		(light) 22% + $3
Trucks	10%	11%	0		20% + $23
					(heavy) 22% + $4
Tires (*% and US$ per 100 kg*)					
Not produced in CA	10% + $10	10% + $10		10% + $10	10% + $10
Produced in CA (under 20 kg)	10% + $90	10% + $90	$75	10% + $90	10% + $90
Produced in CA (over 20 kg)	10% + $75	10% + $75		10% + $75	10% + $75
Jeep Landrover	10	11	0		
Motorcycles (CA assembly)	40% + $25	40% + $25	40% + $25	40% + $25	40% + $25
General License Duties (*US$*)					
Passengers	30	16	New 75, 1 yr old 60, 2 yr old 50, 3 yr old 40, 4 yr old 30, 5 yr old or more 25	$33	$20–30[b]
For rent (6 seats)	35	17 (taxis)			
For rent (12 seats)	38				

Trucks and buses (US$)

Under 1 ton	35 Gasoline (diesel)	16 (30)[c]	New 22	(Trucks) $40	(Trucks) $22 (Buses)[e] $32–45
1–2 tons	43	20 (40)[d]	1 yr old 18	(Buses) $49	25
2–3 tons	58	30 (60)	2 yr old 15		35
3–4 tons	98	40 (100)	3 yr old 12		35
4–5 tons	118	60 (140)	4 yr old 9		35
5–6 tons	138	80 (180)	5 yr old 7		45
6–7 tons	158	100 (220)			55
7–8 tons	178	120 (260)			55
8–9 tons	198	140 (300)			55
9–10 tons	218	160 (340)			60
10–12 tons	238	200 (420)			70
12–15 tons	258	260 (540)			85

Trailers without motor (US$)

	19 (under 4 tons)	until 0.75 tons	6	
	24 (over 4 tons)	1–2 tons	16	
		2–3 tons	30	
		each add. ton	20	

Motorcycles (US$) 13.85   no charge   —   —

Consumption

Passenger Cars (% and US$)			
Up to 2,500	6.5	10	$625–3,160[f]
Over 2,500		20	
Jeep Landrovers	5		$390
Tires			$4–7 (passenger car)
			$5–9 (trucks)[g]

Car Registration Fees (US$)

All categories	Included under Import Duties	On time 5	$5
		Annual 3	

Municipal License Duties (US$)

Passenger cars	Included under General License Duties	7.50
Trucks		12.50

Source: Official publications of governments.

[a] March 6, 1968.
[b] Depending on "fiscal capacity" (FC = .062 × Brake horse-power × cylinder diameter²).
[c] Under 0.75 tons.
[d] 0.75–2 tons.
[e] Depending on number of seats.
[f] Depending on weight.
[g] Depending on size.

79

ship and not upon vehicle kilometers or use of the road system. (It is precisely this feature, of course, that makes this tax more attractive as a revenue device.)

License fees and congestion costs

The more restrictive the license fee the closer it can approximate the costs. The toll (discussed below) is best at approximating congestion costs, but unfortunately the costs of collection are often prohibitive.[32] There is, however, a wide range of possibilities between the toll and the unrestricted license which may serve to approximate some of the costs, particularly congestion costs. For example, licenses can be required for certain routes at certain times. Some of these possibilities are discussed further in Chapter VII.

Tolls

With the exception of the Atlantic Highway and the Quetzaltenango-Champerico road in Guatemala, a bridge over the Ulua River between San Pedro Sula and Tela in Honduras and the Expressway to the airport in San Jose, Costa Rica, no tolls are charged on Central American highways. The few tolls in existence are quite substantial however. In Guatemala on the Atlantic Highway they amount to $.40 per passenger car and $.20 per axle of cargo vehicles for a distance of about 200 km. The bridge toll in Honduras is $.50 for passenger cars and between $1.50 and $3.00 for trucks depending on weight. In Costa Rica the rate is $.13 per passenger car and $.13 per axle for trucks. Both in Costa Rica and Guatemala revenues collected from tolls are relatively low—accounting for between 2 and 3 percent of total revenues collected from road taxes. No revenue data are available for Honduras.

The effects of tolls in terms of their incidence on veh/km are quite substantial, especially if one considers that they are an addition to the other road taxes generally levied. In the case of the Atlantic Highway in Guatemala tolls increase the level of user charges by about 10 percent for a 7-ton truck, 15 percent for a passenger car and a one-ton truck and almost 50 percent for an 18-ton truck. The Atlantic Highway is one of the most important highways in the country since it links the capital with the major port. Since there is, except for the railroad port, no alternative access to Guatemala from the Atlantic side, the toll probably has not had too heavy an impact on through traffic except to protect the railroad which runs parallel. However, very little agricultural or urban development seems to have taken place along the Atlantic

---

[32] Even where the collection costs (both to the authority and the user) are not high, the toll is often inappropriate. The limited access uncongested freeway is a case in point.

Highway in the area close to Guatemala City.[33] In contrast, development is quite intensive along the Pan American Highway which crosses the same general area in the opposite direction. Given the orders of magnitude of toll charges, it is quite conceivable that they contribute substantially to discouraging agricultural development along the Atlantic Highway.

License fees and revenue raising

In contrast to most taxes generally classified in the road user category, license fees have only an indirect incidence on the users of roads. They are more accurately a tax on ownership of property rather than a tax on the use of roads. This indirect incidence makes license fees a more attractive tax for raising revenues than do most other road taxes.

If they are to be used to provide public revenues, the criteria for evaluating license fees must be similar to that for all other tax measures. Consideration must be given to equity, administrative convenience, economic efficiency, etc. One possible criteria that can be adopted is to levy the tax where the demand is most inelastic, possibly for private automobiles in general or on vehicles used in congested urban areas. Equity considerations can be introduced by making the tax higher and perhaps progressively higher on passenger automobiles of greater value.

Other than in Honduras where relatively higher license duties are applied on passenger vehicles, it is difficult to see any application of these general tax criteria to license fees. License fees are highest on large commercial vehicles[34] where the incidence of the tax is likely to cause the greatest loss in economic efficiency and where the greatest possibilities of substitution (via smaller vehicles) exist. These high duties on a small proportion of the vehicle population help to account for the low revenue.

License fees may offer a wide range of opportunities for raising revenues, but unless some care is taken in selecting the base for these taxes an equally wide range of opportunities exist for introducing distortions that will decrease the efficiency of transportation. High taxes on large trucks can encourage the use of smaller less efficient vehicles.[35] Similarly higher taxes on passenger cars

---

[33] This is because the toll does not vary with distance but is a flat rate for entering the highway. The incidence of the toll per vehicle/kilometer is thus very high just beyond the toll gate.

[34] The logic of this traditional structure lies in the argument that heavier vehicles require greater capital expenditures on highways as well as higher maintenance costs. To attempt to recoup capital expenditures in this fashion assumes that the benefits occur to the owners of heavy vehicles. As was pointed out in Chapter II, this is an incorrect view of the incidence of the tax.

[35] There is, for example, a noticeable difference in the fuel types of the heavy truck fleets of Guatemala (25% diesel) and Costa Rica (75% diesel).

81

TABLE 5.7: Fuel Taxes and Prices in the Capital Cities[a]

(US cents per gallon)

	Guatemala			El Salvador			Honduras			Nicaragua			Costa Rica	
	Reg.	Pre-mium	Die-sel	Reg.	Pre-mium	Die-sel	Reg.	Pre-mium	Die-sel	Reg.	Pre-mium	Die-sel	Reg.	Die-sel
Pumphead Price	46.0	49.0	26.0	48.0	51.6	20.0–23.6	45.0	50.0	27.5	42.6	46.4	22.9	41.5	19.2
Taxes	22.2	22.2	5.3	25.7	25.7	2.6	19.8	19.8	3.5	17.0	18.5	3.3	22.3	0
Pumphead Price ex Tax	23.8	27.8	20.7	22.3	25.9	17.4–21.0	25.2	30.2	24.0	25.6	27.9	19.6	19.2	19.2
Approximate Transportation Costs	1.5	1.5	1.5	1.2	1.2	1.2	2.0	2.0	2.0	[b]	[b]	[b]	1.2	1.2
Retail Margin	6.7	7.6	6.4	6.0	7.0	5.4	6.0	7.0	2.5	5.2	5.6	3.7	5.2	5.7
Distributor Margin	7.2	7.4	5.7	5.0	6.2	5.8	17.2	21.2	19.5	20.4	22.3	15.9	4.2	3.5
Refining Prices	8.4	10.3	7.1	10.2	12.1	8.6							8.6	8.8

Source: Petroleum distributors and retailers.
[a] March 6, 1968.
[b] Crude oil transport costs to refinery included in refinery price + distributor margin.

TABLE 5.8: Taxes and Prices for United States and Central American Manufactured Nylon Tires

(US$)

Tire Size (1)	US Produced ex Tax (2)	Honduras		Rest of Central America		
				US Produced		C.A. Produced
		Tax (3)	Retail Price (4) (2 + 3)	Tax (5)	Retail Price (6) (2 + 5)	Retail Price (7)
Passenger Cars						
775–14	25.93	8.85	34.78	13.21	39.14	38.01
815–15	28.53	9.23	37.76	13.92	42.45	39.38
Trucks						
700–16	25.96	10.88	36.84	15.65	41.61	40.73
750–16	32.54	12.98	45.52	18.82	51.36	46.95
750–20	51.43	17.03	68.46	22.17	73.60	82.73
900–20	76.14	27.30	103.44	34.91	111.05	112.00
1,100–20	115.52	36.45	151.97	48.00	163.52	167.00
1,100–20	127.07	40.88	167.95	53.59	180.66	188.60

Source: Price lists Goodyear and GINSA; Central American Common Tariff, Honduran Tariff.

with higher power/weight ratios (generally also the more expensive cars) can increase congestion by encouraging the use of lower-powered vehicles. The use of cheaper vehicles can mean that uneconomic repairs (usually not taxed at the same rate) take place.[36]

License fees will raise average costs in a competitive trucking industry and their incidence is likely to be widespread. Goods and services transported will be affected in accordance with their different elasticities of demand for transport (and consequently the producers and consumers of these goods and services).

Different fees for different types of vehicles will affect the composition of the vehicle fleet and ultimately investment costs. Low fees on heavy trucks will call for heavier road beds with consequent higher costs. Part of this expense can, of course, be avoided by controlling vehicle axle weights.[37]

---

[36] High fuel taxes have similar effects.

[37] This emphasizes the importance of not only the level of road user charges but also their composition in the making of investment decisions. The type of road to be built depends on the type of vehicles to be used, which in turn depends on the type of taxes placed upon these vehicles. Here (as always) the *EUC* is both sufficient and necessary. If the *EUC* is levied it will determine the most efficient form of the vehicle fleet—weight limitations are achieved by heavy vehicles being required to pay for all damages to the road. Faced with these real costs the road user will maximize his benefits. (Footnote continued on page 85)

TABLE 5.9: Road User Charges in Central America for Typical Vehicles and Road Surfaces

		Guatemala			El Salvador		
		Paved	Gravel	Earth	Paved	Gravel	Earth
Average Passenger Car	*Total*	1.839	2.446	3.348	1.641	2.073	2.819
Fuel		.472	.566	.662	.544	.653	.763
Tires		.037	.155	.296	.037	.155	.296
Import duties		.960					
Sales taxes		.170	1.730	2.390	.960	1.270	1.760
License fees		.200			.110		
Toll-Atlantic Highway		(.2 to .3)					
One-Ton Truck Gasoline	*Total*	1.263	1.760	2.616	1.231	1.684	2.426
Fuel		.644	.746	.848	.742	.860	.978
Tires		.039	.144	.318	.039	.144	.318
Import duties		.270			.310		
License fees		.310	.870	1.450	.140	.680	1.130
Toll-Atlantic Highway		(.1 to .2)					
7-Ton Truck Gasoline	*Total*	2.442	3.556	5.370	2.636	3.778	5.589
Fuel		1.722	2.135	2.565	1.986	2.462	2.959
Tires		.150	.566	1.380	.150	.566	1.380
Import duties		.280	.420	.700	.310	.465	.775
License fees		.290	.435	.725	.190	.285	.475
Toll-Atlantic Highway		(.1 to .2)					
7-Ton Truck Diesel	*Total*	1.031	1.817	3.405	1.062	1.900	3.527
Fuel		.271	.336	.500	.132	.164	.197
Tires		.150	.566	1.380	.150	.566	1.380
Import duties		.320	.480	.800	.360	.540	.900
License fees		.290	.435	.725	.420	.630	1.050
Toll-Atlantic Highway		(.1 to .2)					
18-Ton Truck Diesel	*Total*	1. 88	2.837	5.696	1.372	2.982	6.042
Fuel		.363	.497	.631	.177	.242	.307
Tires		.375	1.510	3.685	.375	1.510	3.685
Import duties		.310			.340		
License fees		.240	.830	1.380	.480	1.230	2.050
Toll-Atlantic Highway		(.3 to .5)					

Source: Jan de Weille: Quantification of Road User Savings (basic assumptions regarding annual km, lifetime km, price, etc.).

Assumptions:

(1)	Passenger Car	1-Ton Truck	7-Ton Truck Gas	7-Ton Truck Diesel	18-Ton Truck
Average service life, years	14	12	8	8	7
Average annual km	15,000	14,000	62,000	75,000	112,000
Lifetime km (1 × 2)	210,000	170,000	500,000	600,000	784,000
Price, cif, $	2,200	2,900	10,000	14,000	18,000

(cents per veh/km)

Honduras			Nicaragua			Costa Rica		
Paved	Gravel	Earth	Paved	Gravel	Earth	Paved	Gravel	Earth
1.548	2.045	2.773	1.498	2.018	2.781	3.974	5.261	7.309
.422	.505	.590	.361	.433	.505	.472	.566	.662
.026	.110	.203	.037	.155	.296	.056	.216	.445
.260						1.870		
.400	1.430	1.980	.880	1.430	1.980	1.410	4.479	6.202
.440			.220			.166		
.725	.958	1.306	1.011	1.434	2.167	1.988	2.605	3.565
.514	.665	.756	.492	.570	.649	.644	.746	.848
.031	.113	.250	.039	.144	.318	.047	.173	.383
			.270			1.140		
.120	.180	.300	.210	.720	1.200	.157	1.686	2.334
1.654	2.366	3.405	2.099	3.146	4.920	2.760	3.933	5.759
1.536	1.904	2.288	1.319	1.635	1.965	1.722	2.135	2.565
.117	.447	1.092	.150	.566	1.380	.178	.678	1.654
–	–	–	.560			.770		
.001	.015	.025	.070	.945	1.575	.090	1.120	1.540
.294	.680	1.442	1.009	1.810	3.375	1.908	1.868	3.304
.176	.218	.325	.169	.209	.252	0	0	0
.117	.447	1.092	.150	.566	1.380	.178	.678	1.654
–	–	–	.640			.850		
.001	.015	.025	.050	1.035	1.725	.070	1.190	1.650
.530	1.518	3.416	1.251	2.795	5.703	1.315	2.918	6.005
.236	.323	.411	.226	.310	.393	0	0	0
.293	1.180	2.980	.375	1.510	3.685	.435	1.754	4.421
			.610			.790		
.001	.015	.025	.040	.975	1.625	.090	1.144	1.584

The incidence of vehicle import duties and sales taxes (cost of depreciation) was calculated by assuming that depreciation was caused entirely by use and not time: $ amount of tax was divided by lifetime-km. In addition interest cost was calculated by assuming vehicle was on average depreciated by one-half. 10 percent interest was applied on one-half the vehicle's original value. This amount was divided by annual veh/km in order to get at the tax incidence per veh/km.

(2) It is assumed that the vehicles are running at an average speed of 40 km/h.

To summarize, the license fee offers a wide range of opportunities for pricing road services and as a device for a general taxation. Many of the forms of license duties possible have not been adequately exploited by most countries, but this should be no reason for rejecting them. Many forms (such as some of those discussed in Chapter VII) do appear to be feasible even in a relatively underdeveloped economy. In any case, considerable care is required in levying license fees because of their widespread and often indirect incidence.

Other Minor Duties

In addition to fuel, license, purchase and tire taxes numerous other minor levies are exacted. Taxes on lubricants can reflect use of the road, but as compared with tire and fuel taxes their relationship to use is even more highly variable, while because of their unimportance in total expenditures they form a poor base for raising revenues. Other minor taxes that also have an impact on the price of transport are taxes on drivers, duties on insurance policies, taxes on transfer of vehicle ownership, etc. Their incidence on the cost of transport per mile, on the composition of the vehicle population and on investment decisions should be considered. In the case of Central America, however, these duties are so small that detailed analysis is unnecessary; it is conceivable that in some instances they require more careful handling, as, for example, high license fees for drivers which could have the effect of restricting entry into certain types of carriage. Such cases do not appear to exist in Central America.

VI

THE ECONOMIC COSTS
OF THE OVERPRICING OF THE
UNCONGESTED HIGHWAY

Road Taxes and the Cost of Using the Uncongested Road System

Road taxes and the economic user charge

The system of road user charges that follows from the analysis of this study is one in which the user of the road pays the economic costs of using the road; that is, the user pays what was defined in Chapter II as the economic user charge. In the non-congested rural areas this charge should equal the variable maintenance cost resulting from the passage of the vehicle. The current system of user charges in Central America does not approximate the price required to optimize the allocation of resources; in general, the price is too high in rural areas and too low in urban areas.[1]

Changes are required if the price of using uncongested roads is to approach the costs. The following comparison between costs and prices in Guatemala is reasonably typical for all countries.[2]

---

[1] This is, of course, a general observation. It is difficult to be precise as to the amount of overpricing or underpricing because of the great variation in the incidence of road taxes with vehicle types and road surfaces.

[2] For other countries see data in Chapter V.

TABLE 6.1: User Costs and Charges on Uncongested Roads in Guatemala

(US cents per veh/km)

	Cost	User Charges	User Charges as a Percentage of Costs
Average Passenger Car			
Paved	0.1	1.8	1,800
Gravel	1.1	2.4	218
Dirt	3.3	3.3	100
7-Ton Truck (Gasoline)			
Paved	0.1	2.4	2,400
Gravel	1.1	3.5	318
Dirt	3.3	5.4	164
7-Ton Truck (Diesel)			
Paved	0.1	1.0	1,000
Gravel	1.1	1.8	164
Dirt	3.3	3.4	103

Source: Table 5.9.

In the case of paved roads current user charges exceed the economic costs of using the uncongested paved highways by substantial amounts (particularly for large gasoline trucks). There are a number of qualifications which must be attached to these general conclusions. In the first place they apply largely to paved roads. On unpaved highways the results are not so clear-cut; there are large (but unknown) margins of error in both the cost estimates and the tax incidence. The difficulties in devising a system of user charges to approximate different road surface conditions are such that it is probably better to aim at pricing for the most important type of surface and accept the losses entailed by under (or over) pricing the smaller fraction of the vehicle kilometers on other surfaces. In most of the Central American countries this means pricing to approximate the costs of using paved roads since this is where two-thirds of the vehicle kilometers are traveled. This fraction is likely to grow over time as traffic volumes increase and as roads are improved. Thus focusing attention on paved roads where the results are reasonably clear is likely to introduce the least bias.

A second qualification that must be made concerns the cost estimates. These cost estimates do not differentiate between vehicle types. This is probably incorrect; there is evidence (see Chapter IV) that variable maintenance costs vary with the weight of the vehicle, but no empirical evidence is available to demonstrate this.[3] The quality and quantity of the data in Central America

---

[3] This question has been asked in both the U.S. and the United Kingdom and some research has been done. The results, however, have never been made public.

TABLE 6.2: Vehicle Operating Costs and User Charges, 7-Ton Gasoline Truck and 18-Ton Diesel Truck on Paved Roads

(US cents per veh/km)

	7-Ton Gasoline Truck				18-Ton Diesel Truck			
	Oper-ating Costs	User Charges	Total Costs	Charges as % of Total	Oper-ating Costs	User Charges	Total Costs	Charges as % of Total
Guatemala	6.94	2.44	9.38	26	9.41	1.19	10.60	11
El Salvador	6.94	2.64	9.58	28	9.41	1.37	10.78	13
Honduras	6.94	1.65	8.59	19	9.41	0.53	9.94	5
Nicaragua	6.94	2.01	8.95	22	9.41	1.25	10.66	12
Costa Rica	6.94	2.76	9.70	28	9.41	1.32	10.73	12

Source: Tables 5.9 and 3.7.

was insufficient to permit any estimates of this differential. The "average" costs obtained are thus likely to overestimate the costs for light vehicles and underestimate them for heavy vehicles. The differential between light and heavy vehicles would have to be of very large magnitudes (20 times) to upset the conclusion that some (trucks) vehicle kilometers on paved roads are over priced.

A third point that should be noted is that congestion costs occur at all volumes of traffic. Congestion is a continuous function of volume; even on what are considered "uncongested" roads some congestion occurs. These costs are, however, trivial even in relation to the level of the variable maintenance costs at speeds above 30 kph or traffic flows of less than 100 vehicles per hour. Omitting these congestion costs from the costs of non-urban traffic makes no significant difference to the economic user charge.

User charges and the price of transport

The next point to examine is the extent to which transport prices will be affected by changes in user charges. The demand for transport is a function of the total price of transport, not just the user charge. Table 6.2 shows the magnitude of current user charges within the total cost structure of transport for two typical types of cargo vehicles used in Central America.[4]

For a 7-ton gasoline truck user charges constitute between 19 and 28 percent of the total cost, for an 18-ton diesel truck between 5 and 13 percent. The 18-ton diesel truck is not representative of the typical truck used to haul

---

[4] The estimate of user charges is likely to be on the low side if lower assumptions are made with respect to annual kilometers and vehicle service life. These lower assumptions would raise the percentage of user charges in total costs by less than 5 percent.

agricultural commodities. The model diesel truck has a capacity of seven tons or less, but unfortunately data are not available on the operating costs and technical characteristics of this type of truck.[5] Some idea of the bias introduced by using the data for the larger truck can be obtained. In Table 5.9 estimates of the user charges on a 7-ton diesel truck were made—1.03 cents a vehicle kilometer on paved roads in Guatemala. Assuming the operating costs are 10 percent below those of the 7-ton gasoline truck, say 6.2 cents a vehicle kilometer, the user charge is then 17 percent of the total cost. The lower the operating costs of diesel trucks the higher will be the user charges as a percentage of total price. Taking this into account suggests that 20 percent of the total cost of transport represents the tax element.

Almost all of this represents a discriminatory user charge, that is, a levy over and above the costs of providing the service. Even taking into account the probability that heavy vehicles do, for example, three times more damage than an average vehicle, the discriminatory user charge would be still about 20 percent of the total price of transport. Thus, reducing the level of user charges to that of the economic user charge will reduce transport costs in rural areas (on the assumption of a competitive trucking industry) by 20 percent.

Some qualifications are necessary to take into account the user charge and cost differentials on non-paved highways. The current system of user charges is such that the proportional user charge does not vary very much with the type of road surface. The variable maintenance costs increase substantially as the quality of the surface deteriorates. The net result is that overpricing is less of a problem on dirt and gravel roads than on paved roads. The following figures are for Guatemala but are representative of the other countries as well. (US cents per vehicle kilometer.)

7-Ton Gasoline Truck	Paved	Gravel	Dirt
Vehicle Operating Cost	6.94	9.94	15.65
User Charges	2.44	3.56	5.37
Total Costs	9.38	13.50	21.02
Charges as a % of Total Costs	26	26	26
Discriminatory User Charge[a] as % of Total Costs	25	20	11

[a] Based on variable maintenance cost estimates of 0.1, 1.1 and 3.3 US cents per veh/km (see Chapter IV).

On gravel roads charges still exceed variable maintenance costs by a significant percentage. For dirt roads the percentage is cut in half. If user charges

[5] The primary source of the technical coefficients and cost information is data from the more developed countries where a 7-ton diesel truck is not typical.

were reduced so that total transport costs were cut by roughly 20 percent,[6] the result would not be a subsidy for users of gravel roads, but a subsidy of about 10 percent of price for users of dirt roads.[7]

The current system of user charges thus increases the price of transport by about 20 percent more than would be the case if economic user charges were levied. The question of how much this policy costs in terms of resource allocation can now be rephrased slightly to ask what would happen if transport costs were reduced 20 percent.

The Elasticity of Demand for Transport: Theoretical Considerations

In order to calculate the effects of a change in transport prices it is necessary to know the response of traffic to the price of transport. What goods will move and in what quantity will depend on the elasticity of demand for transport services. It is only in the extreme case where the demand is perfectly inelastic that price does not affect the tonnage of traffic. On the basis of the available evidence this extreme is difficult to defend; the more likely probability is that most demand curves have some elasticity. The question is how much.

The estimation of demand elasticities is no simple matter. Extreme problems of identification exist; it is difficult to distinguish movements along the demand curve from shifts in the demand curve—i.e., to separate out the effects of changes in price from the effects of everything else. Even in developed countries where a great deal of data exist, the statistical measurement of demand curves for transport has not provided reliable estimates.

The difficulties associated with directly estimating demand elasticities suggest that it may be better to approach the problem indirectly. This can be done by specifying the nature of the production function and the demand for the output. The derived demand for transport can then be calculated. To do this for every commodity transported is, of course, a monumental task and one which would be unlikely to yield benefits in excess of costs. Some simplification is therefore desirable.

This chapter will consider a simplified model of agricultural development and how this can be used to make meaningful statements concerning the elasticity of demand for transport of agricultural goods.[8] This type of model

---

[6] It is assumed here that it is not possible to devise a system of user charges that would accurately reflect costs for all types of road surfaces, and because of the predominance of vehicle kilometers on paved roads, it is better to aim at approximating the price for this surface.

[7] This may not be undesirable when both equity and efficiency are considered.

[8] The model that follows is based upon the model of development first put forward by Charles Ellet in 1836. This model has been more fully developed by

is particularly relevant in the context of Central America, which is primarily rural with a large and important agricultural sector. It is in the agricultural sector with its output of high bulk, low value commodities that high elasticities of demand for transport and thus high costs of over-pricing are likely to be found.

The basic model

In its simplest form this model assumes that in a given country, bordered by a coastline in a North-South direction, all land is homogeneous. One single (export) product is grown for which at the port the demand elasticity is infinite. The farmer can sell any quantity at the going (world market) price. The rules of transport allow that goods are transported either parallel to the coast line (North-South) or at a right angle from the port into the interior (East-West). Before the road is constructed transport takes place in the form of headloading. After the road is built the product is transported by a combination of headloading and road transport. For both modes it is assumed that costs per ton/kilometer are constant. In this simplest form of the model it is also assumed that the length of the road is not limited (the road goes as far as there is any development). It is further assumed that the cost of inputs other than land needed to produce one unit of output are constant.

If k is the market price at the port, f the cost of other inputs, b the cost of headloading per ton/kilometer, the production per hectare is one ton, and x and y are the coordinates to describe the location of the farm in the interior, then the area of cultivation without the road (see Figure 1) must meet the following conditions:

$$k - f = b(x + y) \text{ for } y \geq 0$$
$$k - f = b(x - y) \text{ for } y \leq 0$$

As long as for any hectare of land the rent value $k - f - b(x + y)$ $[y \geq 0]$ is positive, the land which will be cultivated corresponds to the triangle ABJ. in Figure 1.

If a road is constructed and a represents the ton/km cost of road transport, the area of cultivation will be described by:

$$k - f = ax + by \, [y \geq 0]$$
$$k - f = ax - by \, [y \leq 0]$$

Alan Walters in *The Economics of Road User Charges*, World Bank Staff Occasional Paper No. 5. (Baltimore: The Johns Hopkins Press, 1968), Chapter V. Only the simple version of the Ellet model is considered here. The model can be subject to considerable sophistication and for this the reader is referred to Walters' discussion.

FIGURE 1
MAP OF CULTIVATED AREA WITH
ENDLESS ROAD

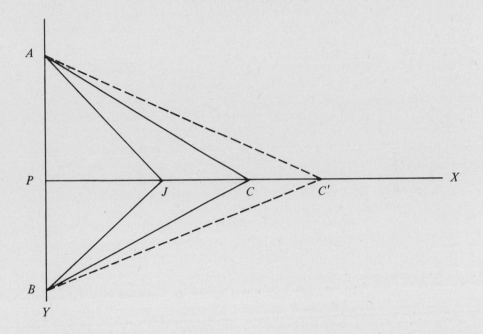

Again, if $k - f - ax - by$ $[y \geq 0]$ has a positive value, land will be cultivated. The new triangle is limited by ABC. Production has been extended along the new highway. The distances PA, PB and PC are easy to determine. In the case of PA and PB all products are headloaded. The distance (y) therefore is $\dfrac{k - f}{b}$ km. In the case of PC the total production is transported by truck. Hence $x = \dfrac{k - f}{a}$ km.

The task is now to find the elasticity of demand for road transport along the road. Let transport costs on the road (e.g., as a result of paving) be reduced from a per ton/km to $a(1- \lambda)$ per ton/km, where $1 > \lambda > 0$. Therefore λ represents the proportional reduction in transport costs as a result of the road improvement. Analogous to what was described above, the result of a fall in transport costs will be a further extension of production along the highway to C' (see Figure 1.) The distance PC' amounts to $\dfrac{k - f}{a(1 -\lambda)}$ km and the new

93

area of cultivation is described by:

$$k - f \leq a(1 - \lambda)x + by \ [y \geq 0] \text{ and}$$
$$k - f \geq a(1 - \lambda)x - by \ [y \leq 0]$$

Elasticities of demand for transport can be defined either in terms of tons or ton/kilometers. In the simpler case of tons carried, the proportionate increase in production (area) amounts to:[9]

$$\frac{\lambda}{1 - \lambda}$$

With a proportionate change of price of $- \lambda$, the elasticity of demand for transport in terms of tons (ϵ tons) will be:

$$\epsilon \text{ tons} = \lim_{\lambda \to 0} \frac{-1}{1 - \lambda} = -1$$

Thus a 10 percent decrease in the price of transport will increase the area of cultivation by 10 percent. Similarly it can be shown, that the elasticity for transport demand in terms of ton/kilometers is -2.[10]

The results are very simple, but this was achieved by using some simplifying assumptions. Changing the assumptions will change the results. The following are the basic assumptions of the model:

a) Demand for output[11] is perfectly elastic;
b) Supply of factors is perfectly elastic;
c) Land is homogeneous in quality;
d) Headloading is at right angles to the road;
e) Transport costs per ton/kilometer are constant.

A change in most of these assumptions will usually lower the elasticity of demand for transport. At the extreme, if either the supply of factors and/or the demand for output is perfectly inelastic so will be the demand for the tonnage of goods for transport. (But the redistribution of production will increase the number of ton/kilometers.) Similarly, land of decreasing quality, increasing transport costs per ton/kilometer, and non-competitive conditions in either the markets for factors or for products will each decrease the elasticity of demand for transport. The assumption that headloading takes place at right

---

[9] Area of cultivation before improvement is $\dfrac{(k - f)^2}{ab}$, after improvement $\dfrac{(k - f)^2}{ab \ (1 - \lambda)}$.

[10] For calculation see Walters, p. 152.

[11] Only one commodity has been considered. The introduction of more commodities increases the number of development triangles but does not change the results.

angles to the road simplifies the mathematics but does not materially change the results.[12]

How relevant are these assumptions in the case of Central America? In general they appear to be realistic, particularly if the time period considered is of sufficient length to allow adjustments to take place. The smaller the area considered the more realistic the assumptions are likely to be.

The most important assumptions are those concerning the supply of factors and the demand for output. The assumption of perfectly elastic demand for the product at the port is probably sensible for a number of agricultural commodities produced in Central America. In the case of export products, with the relatively small shares of Central American producers in total world supply, the producer can probably sell as much as he can produce at the going world price without influencing the price. For certain commodities the total quantity is limited by quota arrangements (e.g., coffee). In the case of an agricultural commodity for consumption in a domestic market, the assumption of a perfectly elastic demand is less realistic. Nevertheless, there are situations where the demand for an agricultural commodity from a particular area is perfectly elastic because of the availability of alternative imported supplies at fixed prices. If the total demand is exclusively satisfied from domestic production and if there are no exports from the area, a further increase in output would lead to a decrease in price.

Arguments for a fairly elastic supply curve of factors (at least for labor) can also be made along similar lines. Rural underemployment should generally mean this factor can be provided at approximately constant costs. The elasticity of the supply of land may be a more debatable point. Diminishing returns due to the decline in the quality of soil may be partly mitigated by technological developments which improve the productivity of poorer soils.

The assumptions can be changed to fit the reality of a particular situation. Divergences from the simplified assumptions used here will usually decrease the elasticity of demand for transport.[13] The figures -1 for tons and -2 for ton/kilometers can normally be considered as maximum values. The impact of changing these elasticities on the benefits of a change in transport prices is discussed later in this chapter.

The Development Model: Some Empirical Evidence

The complexities that are introduced into the simple model by the particular circumstances of a specific case greatly increase the amount of data needed.

---

[12] See Walters, Annex to Chapter IV.

[13] Sometimes one may argue that the elasticity will be increased; one such example is where there are returns to scale in marketing.

Much of this data is available only after extensive reworking of the raw material—a task beyond the time and scope of this study. Fortunately one fairly simple case could be found, that of the Western Highway in Honduras. The conditions are approximately those of the simple model: an endless road (for practical purposes) with one market and a homogeneous pattern of cultivation (corn and beans). Agricultural censuses covering the periods both before and after the improvement in the road are available and the census units are small enough to yield meaningful results.

The Western Highway in Honduras

Since 1955 the Western Highway has been improved in various stages from an earth road usable only in the dry season to a well-aligned gravel road. In 1950 the road extended from San Pedro Sula to Santa Rosa de Copan over a total length of 170 km. Between 1962 and 1966 the road was extended from Santa Rosa to the Salvadorian Border at Ocotepeque in order to provide a through connection from the industrial center around San Pedro and the Atlantic port in Cortes to the city of San Salvador and the port on the Pacific coast. Except for a section between La Entrada and Santa Rosa, the improvement of the original road was roughly completed in 1962. A substantial part of the impact of the road on agricultural development should therefore show up in the 1965/66 census data used in the calculations below. This is not the case for the extension of the Western Highway beyond Santa Rosa, as this was only opened to traffic in 1965.

For most of its length the road follows a valley of varying width and twice crosses a sizeable mountain range (once between La Entrada and Santa Rosa and once between Santa Rosa and Ocotepeque). To the casual observer the land seems to be about equally suitable throughout the entire length of the road for cultivation of corn and beans, the two major agricultural commodities produced in the area. Nevertheless, the assumption of homogeneous land is a rough approximation of reality since yields per hectare are likely to decrease as production extends beyond the valley into the hills and mountains. Transport from the farms to the Western Highway is mainly by donkey and in some cases by four-wheel drive vehicles, since in the past only a few feeder roads existed in the area of influence of the road. It was only after 1964 that a major feeder road construction program was initiated.

The pattern of cultivation

The special characteristics of the Honduran case and the form in which the data are presented make it necessary to modify the basic endless road model. Since it is impossible to separate subsistence from market production a "subsistence corridor" parallel to the road is needed. The subsistence corridor

FIGURE 2
MAP OF CULTIVATED AREA WITH
SUBSISTENCE FARMING

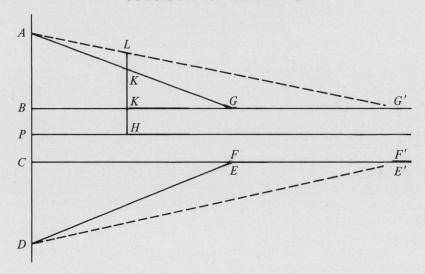

represents the production that would have taken place even if no road had ever been built; that is, settlement usually occurs along the valley bottom and the same location is generally used for roads. In most of Honduras some form of subsistence farming takes place in areas remote from the road network.

This is illustrated in Figure 2. Instead of one market production triangle, two triangles (ABG and CDE) extend from the end of the "subsistence corridor" on both sides. The further assumption is made that the subsistence corridor extends all the way from San Pedro to Santa Rosa (at the physical end of the road).[14] Such a shape is not unreasonable since the population in the various groups of municipalities (except for the market in San Pedro) is roughly the same and hence about the same amount of subsistence food production can be expected. While the physical end of the road is in Santa Rosa, the "end of the road" as far as market production is concerned might be closer to the market, the distance given by the formula: $\dfrac{k-s}{a}$ km, where k is the market price, s the headloading cost from the edge of the subsistence strip to the road, and a the road transport cost per ton/kilometer.[15]

---

[14] Note that the physical end of the road in this case (Santa Rosa) would be beyond F'. The shape of the end-of-the-road triangle would be as outlined in the discussion of the truncated road.

[15] Assuming here that there are no other inputs than transport.

In analogy with the simple endless road case, when the road is improved the market triangles are extended to ABG' and CDE' with increasing growth rates of area cultivated (production) up to G, and from there on decreasing growth rates to the end of the road for market production (G').

In order to verify the shape of the cultivated area and thus the basic assumptions of the model, it would be necessary to have information on the areas cultivated and their distances from the road. It was not possible to obtain this data, but given certain assumptions regarding the pattern of cultivation the data on production can be interpreted as being at least consistent with the assumptions of the model.

Production figures for the area of influence of the Western Highway are available from the agricultural census (1952 and 1965/66) on a municipal level. For the purpose of comparison the municipalities were grouped so that the area of each group of municipalities extended approximately to the same distance from the road (some 10 to 15 kilometers on both sides). This in effect covers an area parallel to the road at a distance PA and PD (see Figure 2). Within this area the following changes in production of corn and beans were observed over the period 1952 to 1965/66. The groups of municipalities are ranked by increasing distance from the main market (San Pedro Sula).

From Table 6.3 it can be seen that the rate of growth of production is consistent with the pattern of cultivation used in the model. Growth rates (in terms of the figure, LK over KH) are low around the market and increase rapidly beyond 130 km (group 4 of the municipalities). There is even the predicted "trailing off" of the growth rate after this point (G in the figure) that can be accounted for by the existence of a subsistence corridor. The end of the road for most of this period was Santa Rosa de Copan (Group 7) and beyond this point, with the exception of Group 10, growth rates drop drastically, picking up again only in Group 12.[16]

The above results could also be consistent with a different pattern of cultivation; that is, the growth could have taken place within the corridor of municipalities but outside the triangles $AG'B$ and $CE'D$ of Figure 2. This is unlikely, however. Observations by the study team tended to confirm the fact that the area of cultivation decreased as distance from San Pedro Sula increased. These observations are supported by the almost negligible rate of growth in municipalities immediately adjacent to those in the areas covered

---

[16] Group 12 can be explained easily. The area around Ocotepeque is a traditional exporter to San Salvador. The road to San Salvador has been improved starting in the early sixties, and moreover El Salvador increasingly became an importer of corn. No information is available as to Group 10, although it appears conceivable that the same explanations as for Group 12 are valid.

TABLE 6.3: Production of Corn and Beans in the Western Region (Honduras) by Groups of Municipalities, 1952 and 1966

Group of Municipalities		Average Distance in km from San Pedro Sula (1)	Production in Quintales (lq = 46 kg)		% of Increase (3)/(2) (4)
			1952 (2)	1966 (3)	
San Pedro	1	0–21	51,885	53,297	2.7
	2	60	67,651	97,092	43.5
	3	72	87,516	173,032	97.7
	4	126	72,461	155,023	113.9
	5	129	117,948	201,090	70.5
	6	131	45,442	76,147	65.6
Santa Rosa	7	170	90,669	123,983	36.7
	8	185	61,210	63,542	3.8
	9	195	40,530	41,639	2.7
	10	210	16,049	19,426	21.0
	11	230	17,654	18,013	2.0
Ocotepeque	12	240	18,584	27,184	46.3

Source: Primero y Segundo Censo Nacional Agropecuario, 1950 and 1965/66.
Groups: No. 1: San Pedro, Villa Nuevo; *No. 2:* Quimistan, Petoa, San Marcos; *No. 3:* Mazuelizo, Azacualpa; *No. 4:* Florida, Nueva Arcadia; *No. 5:* Concepcion, San Antonio, San Geronimo, San Nicolas Trinidad; *No. 6:* Dolores, San Jose, Dulce Nombre, Vera Cruz, Santa Rita (half); *No. 7:* San Juan Opoa, Santa Rosa, Cucuyagua, Talgua, Santa Rita (half); *No. 8:* San Pedro, Corquin, La Union, Cabanas; *No. 9:* Lucerna, San Jorge, Sensenti, San Fernando, La Encarnacion; *No. 10:* Fraternidad, La Labor, San Francisco; *No. 11:* Dolores, Sinuapa, Concepcion; *No. 12:* Nueva Ocotepeque, Santa Fe, Mercedes (half).

by the production data and at the end of the road. Other evidence that supports the interpretation consistent with the model is the visible increase in cultivation that took place when the Western Highway was extended to Ocotepeque in 1965.[17] In 1966 the cultivation of corn beyond Santa Rosa was sporadic; in 1967 most of the terrain adjacent to the road was cultivated with corn, the market in this case being El Salvador.

These observations tend to support the contention of the model that cultivation will take place at decreasing distances from the road as distance from the market increases. This increases the degree of confidence that can be placed in the theoretically predicted values of the elasticity of demand for transport services.

Direct estimate of the elasticity

In addition to verifying the pattern of cultivation predicted by the model, it is possible to make a direct estimate of the demand elasticity. No data are

---

[17] Unfortunately the time from the opening to the agricultural census was less than one year, hence no data are available to support these visual impressions gathered by recent Bank missions.

available on the change in freight rates over the Western Highway before and after the improvement of the road. The de Weille Study suggests that improving an all-weather earth road to a gravel road amounts to a reduction in truck vehicle operating costs of between 37 to 41 percent of the cost before the improvement, depending on truck size. Trucking in Honduras is very competitive; there is free entry and most truck operations are the owner-operator type. Hence one should expect that lower transport costs should be passed on entirely in the form of lower freight rates. In the case of the Western Highway the reduction in vehicle operating costs should be even higher; in 1950 the road was not even an all-weather road and the present gravel road is of very high standard. The improved road is also shorter than the old road, and over these years there have been reductions in relative truck costs as technical progress has taken place in vehicle building. Savings in operating costs are more likely therefore to be on the order of 50 percent.

The proportionate increase in the production of corn and beans in the municipal groups 1–8 (from 594,782 quintales in 1950 to 943,206 quintales in 1965/66[18] amounted to 58 percent. Hence the elasticity of the derived demand for transport in terms of tons was in the neighborhood of unity.[19] If it can be shown that the demand for corn and beans in the market was very elastic, the above results would be consistent with the predictions of the model. Only indirect evidence exists regarding the demand elasticities for the product. Prices for beans and corn in San Pedro have not shown a decreasing trend since 1956 (although annual fluctuations have been quite erratic depending on the harvest); the increasing quantities were sold without lowering prices. This indicates that over the long run the demand for Western Highway corn and beans must have been quite elastic. A further qualification may be made. In the above calculation the total increase in production was attributed to road improvement. Of course there were other influencing factors. In principle the increase in production that would have taken place without the improved road is what should be measured. In the "roadless" areas of Honduras production was almost stagnant over this period. Some of the expansion of production along the Western Highway was undoubtedly diverted from other areas, but the reduction in transport demand in other areas due to the diversion effect is difficult to assess. Probably the increase in production in the Western Highway

---

[18] See Table 6.3.

[19] $\dfrac{\text{Proportionate change in production}}{\text{Proportionate change in transport price}} = \dfrac{58}{-50} = 1.16$

If, however, allowances are made for the production that would have taken place without the road, the numerator would be reduced and the elasticity would be less (in absolute terms).

100

region that would have occurred without the improvements would have been on the order of 20 percent.[20] Thus the ceteris paribus elasticity of demand is $-38/50 = -0.76$.

The Honduran data do not seem to discredit the conclusions of the model. There can be little doubt that road improvement in the Western Region was instrumental in bringing about the increase in production. The order of magnitude of the demand elasticity for road transport (in terms of tons) encountered in the Honduran case is not far from what was predicted by the model. Further empirical verification through similar case studies would strengthen the general applicability of the model, but as a start the Honduran case is promising.

Estimating the Costs of Excessive User Charges

In the case examined it is clear that the demand curve is not absolutely inelastic with respect to the price of transport. In the simple model of agricultural development the estimate of the elasticity in terms of tons was not too far from the theoretically predicted value. The development model is a reasonable characterization of the type of economic activity that takes place in Central America. The region is primarily agricultural, and the transport of high bulk, low value agricultural products accounts for about 40 percent of the volume of highway transport. Thus, changes in the price of transport are likely to affect much of the economic activity.

To examine the precise impact of a decline in transport cost would require a general equilibrium model of the economy. Such a model does not exist, nor is it likely that one having the necessary degree of complexity will be constructed in the future. Reliance must be placed on simpler techniques.

Some idea of the magnitude of the costs of existing policy can be obtained by making some simplified assumptions about the economy and then at a later stage incorporating the more realistic assumptions. Once the demand curve for transport has been calculated (or assumed), it is possible to estimate the increase in output that would result from a lowering of price. In Figure 3 the demand curve for transport is given by DD'. The initial price of transport is given by P_1 and the initial output (in vehicle/kilometers)[21] by Q_1. Lowering

---

[20] The evidence for this conjecture is that the total expansion of production of corn and beans was of the order of 38% (1952–65). Practically all this increase was concentrated in areas which had road improvements. If there had been no road improvement at all in Honduras it is unlikely that the aggregate increase would have much exceeded 20 percent.

[21] Changing the unit of output to ton/kilometers alters the scale at which the demand curve is plotted but not the results. Vehicle/kilometers are used because this is the unit of output most readily available.

FIGURE 3
INCREASE IN OUTPUT WITH LOWER PRICES

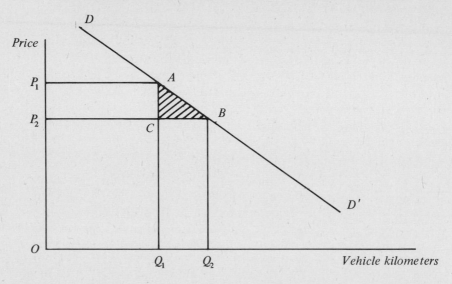

the price to P_2 increases the output to Q_2. The increase in consumer surplus in the transport sector is given by the area $P_1 P_2 B A$. Not all of this is, however, a net addition to output. If the reduction from P_1 to P_2 is the result of lowering user charges from a discriminatory user charge to an economic user charge, the area $P_1 P_2 C A$ represents the tax revenues of the government at price P_1. The net addition to output is given by the area of the triangle ABC.

That this triangle and not the area ABQ_2Q_1 measures the total benefits from the reduction in price should be obvious from the construction of the demand curve. The demand curve assumes that all factors receive a rate of return equal to their opportunity cost. The area CBQ_2Q_1 represents the returns of the increased employment of factors in this industry, but at the rate of return they would have received elsewhere in the economy.[22] In the agricultural case where all factors except land are mobile, the area ABC would represent the increase in land rents.

The area ABC can be estimated very crudely for Central America by giving the demand curve the elasticity estimate derived from both the theoretical and empirical considerations. For agricultural commodities the demand curve can be assumed to be -1 in terms of tons and -2 in terms of ton/kilometers.

---

[22] It is conceivable that the general rate of return of a factor may increase because of the lowering of the price of transport. This point is discussed further below.

Assuming that ton/kilometers and vehicle/kilometers are equivalent,[23] and that a 20 percent change in price is approximately equal to two US cents per veh/km, and that the result would approximate the economic user charge, the following calculation of the area ABC can be made:

TABLE 6.4: **Estimate of Increased Output by Two-Cent Reduction in Transport Price**

	Total Rural veh/km[a] (annual, in millions)	Agricultural veh/km[b] (in millions)	Change in Agricultural veh/km[c]	Area of ABC[d] (million $)
Guatemala	770	313	125	1.25
Honduras	213	86	34	0.34
El Salvador	586	238	95	0.95
Nicaragua	418	170	68	0.68
Costa Rica	488	197	79	0.79
Total		1,004	401	4.01

[a] From Table 3.1.
[b] Based on TSC origin-destination survey of 1964. 40.6 percent of all tons carried were of agricultural and forestry products.
[c] A change in price of 20 percent would mean an increase in output (veh/km) of 40 percent.
[d] One half of .02 × change in agricultural veh/km.

The increased output that would result from lowering transport prices by two cents is thus four million dollars per year, or alternatively the cost of current policy is four million dollars per year. This four million dollars is slightly less than one-tenth of one percent of GDP, or about 10 percent of total user taxes collected from non-congested road use.

This is an extremely crude estimate, but qualifications do not significantly alter its magnitude. The first point to consider is the value of the elasticity of demand for transport. The value of two used here is likely to be a maximum. It is based on the assumption of a perfectly elastic demand for output and a perfectly elastic supply of factors.[24] This is not an unreasonable assumption for an isolated case within the larger framework of the whole economy; that is, it is probably more relevant to a specific project such as the Western Highway in Honduras than to the economy as a whole. Thus it is likely that there will be some inelasticity in both the supply and demand curves for output that would lower the elasticity of demand for transport to less than two and as a result lower the estimate of benefits. This is, however, likely to be the case only in the short run. As the time horizon is lengthened both supply and demand fac-

---

[23] That is, the same load factor is applied.
[24] One of these factors is land. If land were unavailable or of lower quality the elasticity of demand for transport would be reduced correspondingly.

tors will become more elastic and the estimate of the elasticity of the derived demand for transport will approach closer to the theoretical value of two. The benefits may then be thought of as occurring after an interval of time sufficient to allow adjustments to take place. If this time period is five years the annual benefits will approach four million at the end of this period.

The estimate of the loss in agricultural output would be greater if, as was suggested earlier, the incidence on vehicle/kilometers of the license fees and purchase taxes were higher. A reduction by one-third of the assumed vehicle service life and annual kilometers traveled would increase the estimated level of total user charges by an additional 5 percent of total transport costs. This would permit an additional reduction in transport costs of 5 percent, increasing the estimate of the area ABC by 1.25 million dollars. The estimate presented here is thus likely to be on the low side.

A further factor which suggests this figure may be an underestimate is the high probability of the existence of excess supplies of labor. The assumption used in the estimate was that of a fully employed economy. If there is unemployment or underemployed labor (labor that has an opportunity cost of zero or close to it), the increase in output would be in excess of that suggested by the model used here. A simple case may illustrate this point. According to the Government of El Salvador's *Plan Quinquenal de Desarrollo Agropecuario, 1961*, 32.6 percent or 125,000 persons in agriculture were permanently unemployed. A decrease in transport prices of 20 percent would make (on the basis of various assumptions of the model) 20 percent more land available, adding another 19 thousand hectares to cultivation. Using the average figure of 2.5 persons per hectare, this would mean employment opportunities would be opened up for 47,500 persons, or 38 percent of the unemployed. Thus in addition to the rent of area ABC, there would be the labor income of these persons which, at a wage rate of 200 dollars per year, would be an additional 9.5 million dollars or about 1.2 percent of GNP in El Salvador. (In terms of growth rates this would mean an increase in the rate of growth by 25 percent for one year—not an insignificant achievement.) Similar conditions of rural unemployment exist in all the countries of Central America.

Furthermore, the discussion has been confined to agriculture only; additional benefits exist if there is some elasticity of demand in the transport of non-agricultural commodities, which account for 60 percent of the tonnage carried over highways. Unfortunately it is not possible to speculate on the demand elasticities of these various products. On some commodities, particularly finished manufactured products, the elasticity of demand is likely to be quite low as transport costs represent only a small part of total costs. In some cases, however, especially where Central American alternatives exist for previously imported commodities, the elasticity may be considerable—as possibly in the case of cement (see Table 3.8). The net benefits would depend on the natural resource content of the output and the opportunity costs of the other factors employed.

These qualifications suggest that the results be interpreted with a great deal of care. They probably understate the loss in output that results from a policy of user charges in excess of economic costs. It would not be difficult by making reasonably realistic assumptions regarding underemployment, induced non-agricultural traffic, etc. to arrive at an estimate that is close to two percent of GDP. It should be remembered that this increase can be achieved by little or no expenditure of resources. By any standards this would be regarded as a substantial achievement of public policy.

The estimates of the increase in output that could occur have been made within the context of reducing current user charges. The opposite, that of raising user charges, is also a policy option. In this case it would be more accurate to think in terms of the increased loss in output that would follow from such a policy; these estimates are by no means trivial.

VII

URBAN ROADS AND TRANSPORT

Local Government and Urban Street Services

The problem in perspective

A general problem in Latin America has been the financial difficulties experienced by local governments. The traditional pattern inherited from colonial times of small and numerous political units with minor powers of taxation has not been able to deal with the problems inherent in the shift from a rural to an urban society. The difficulties of local government are even more marked in Central America than in most of Latin America. The small size of the countries has made it easier for the central government to expand its base at the expense of local governments. This is not in itself undesirable and may in some cases lead to an improvement in the quality of government services. There are, however, conspicuous failures, not the least of which is the failure to deal with the problems brought on by motor vehicle traffic. Central governments have appropriated the revenues of local governments but not their responsibilities.[1]

In Central America most local governments have declined to levels where they are no longer of much significance. Table 7.1 indicates the position of

---

[1] This is not peculiar to Latin America but is endemic the world over. It seems, however, to be of a greater relative magnitude in Latin America.

TABLE 7.1: Comparison of Central Government and Local Government Revenues in Central America

(million US$)

	Central Government Current Revenues (1966) (1)	Local Government Revenues (2)	Capital City Revenues (3)	(3) as % of (2) (4)
Guatemala	121.0		10.0[a]	
El Salvador	89.5		–	
Honduras	60.2	14.3[b]	3.7[b]	26
Nicaragua		5.4	1.8	33
Costa Rica[c]	85.8	9.3	3.7	40

[a] Budget 1967.
[b] Budget 1968.
[c] 1965 at exchange rate of US$1 = 6.65 colones.

local or municipal governments as compared with that of the central government. The situation in some cases is even more pronounced when the transfers from the central government to local government are taken into account. In Costa Rica over 50 percent of local revenues in the table above are transfers received from the central government. The data also indicate that outside of the capital city in each country, local government is on a very small scale.

It is in these capital cities that most of the typical urban problems are encountered, for once outside them the economies are essentially rural. All of these cities face serious difficulties in meeting the demands made upon them for the provision of urban services. Transportation is only one of these services, but the problems encountered here are typical of those found in the provision of other services. Weak administrations, inadequate taxes, and divided responsibilities are all part of the municipal picture regardless of the service being considered.

The central government of each country has attempted to alleviate some of the problems of their capital cities or metropolitan areas by assuming some functions of local government. In both San Jose and San Salvador the maintenance and construction of urban streets is partly a responsibility of the central government. In San Salvador the responsibility is explicit in that paved urban streets[2] are the responsibility of a dependency of the Ministry of Public Works, the Department of Urbanism and Architecture (DUA). In San Jose the arrangements are more informal with the Ministry of Transport doing occasional work on urban streets. Similar arrangements have been made from time to time in Tegucigalpa, Managua and Guatemala City. The result is usually

---

[2] Unpaved streets being the responsibility of the municipality of San Salvador.

a confusion of responsibilities which ends up with neither level of government doing anything until the situation becomes really desperate.

Local government revenues and urban street expenditures

The weak base on which municipal taxes are levied is very clear; revenues come largely from business license fees, rent of market spaces, sale of municipal services, central government transfers, and taxes shared with the central government. The property tax, which in many countries is the backbone of local taxation, is insignificant. In Costa Rica, Guatemala and Nicaragua the property tax is a national tax. In Costa Rica the local governments receive 15 percent of the property tax collected within their area. In Honduras and El Salvador the property tax is a local tax that is so poorly enforced and administered that little revenue is collected.

Revenues collected from taxes associated with road use also form a minor part of local government revenues. In Costa Rica and El Salvador the local governments receive no taxes from the users of urban streets.[3] In the other countries some revenues are obtained from road users. In Honduras, Guatemala and Nicaragua parts of the annual license duties are earmarked for the municipalities (see page 77) but the rates are low (e.g., $7.50 per car in Honduras) with the result that the revenues are not very significant. In Guatemala and Nicaragua part of the gasoline tax is distributed to the municipalities (see page 69).

Revenues are not commensurate with the responsibilities of local governments in the area of urban road construction and maintenance; given the lack of alternative sources of revenue available to these governments, it is not surprising to find a poor level of road services.

The state of urban streets

Perhaps the most striking feature in all the countries in Central America is the contrast between interurban highways and streets in the city or town. The casual traveler is struck by the fact that one approaches the city on a good well-surfaced road, but when the road reaches the town or city boundary it deteriorates, sometimes to a stretch of mud and usually to a very much inferior surface. Where the traffic is most dense the road is worst.[4] Except for San Salvador the best that can be said about the condition of the streets is that they are poor and show signs of continuous neglect. Perhaps the best example of this neglect is Tegucigalpa, where five to seven thousand vehicles per day

---

[3] See Table 5.6.

[4] One example is on the Salvadorian part of the Western Highway as it passes through La Palma. Another example is the Atlantic Highway, which becomes an unkept track when one enters Guatemala City.

108

Urban Streets and Urban Maintenance Expenditures
(km and million US$)

	Urban Streets			Maintenance Expend. (1968 budget)	Maintenance Expend. Dollars per km
	Paved	Unpaved	Total		
Tegucigalpa				0.246[a]	
San Jose	594	162	756	0.297[b]	388
Guatemala	336	354	690	0.252[c]	360
San Salvador	309	n.a.			

[a] Includes new constructions.
[b] Excludes small amount done by Ministry of Transport.
[c] Expenditures for 1967.

run over streets most of which are unpaved. The figures on maintenance expenditures on urban streets in Table 7.2 indicate the magnitude of the problem.

The condition of urban streets is a good deal worse than is indicated by the data on maintenance expenditures. Construction expenditures are so low as to be almost negligible. The high percentage of unpaved streets within the limits of the metropolitan area are indicative of the long years of neglect. Many of these streets carry sufficient volumes of traffic to justify their paving on the basis of vehicle cost savings alone.

Traffic engineering and enforcement

The second feature in the city streets is the clear need for traffic engineering and more effective policing of traffic regulations. There is no doubt that some of the congestion could be mitigated by the use of "no left turn" signals at suitable intersections, more parking restrictions, additional traffic lights, improved lane markings, etc. In some of the cities the quality of traffic engineering is moderate, but in others such as Tegucigalpa it is poor. It seems that quite a modest expenditure on traffic engineering, together with the widening of certain intersections, could bring proportionally larger benefits without greatly infringing upon the liberty of individual road users.

The enforcement of existing parking and traffic regulations is not as vigorous and not nearly as effective as one finds in North American cities—although it may be claimed to be a fair average for cities in the developing countries. Part of the difficulty lies in legal and constitutional constraints; authorities have few legal sanctions against violators of traffic regulations,[5] and it is often difficult to effect any change by means of the legislative process.

---

[5] For example in San Salvador the municipality has no right to prosecute a person who fails to put proper coins into a parking meter.

Parking

Downtown parking is becoming no less a problem in the major cities of the region that it is in the central business districts (CBD's) of the United States and Europe. Perhaps the most striking difference between the two is the large amount of curbside parking tolerated (either legally or illegally) in the region. Streets in the city centers—laid out long before the motor age—have their capacity cut to a half or even a third by lines of parked vehicles. Although there is no statistical evidence at present available, it seems clear that the majority of parkers are in fact commuters into the central business districts. Only in Guatemala and San Salvador is there metered street parking and even here there are no restrictions on meter feeding.[6] In the other cities curbside parking is free provided that one can find a place.

The pressure of demand for parking space has given rise to various familiar effects. First there is much illegal parking. In San Jose, for example, it was frequently observed that both sides of the street were full of parked vehicles in spite of the fact that legally one could park only on one side. Legal sanctions are scant and not vigorously enforced. Second, even in those cities where curbside parking is free, the difficulty and cost of finding a place are so great that off-street parking lots provided by private enterprises have grown rapidly.[7]

Parking capacity varies considerably from the lowest in Tegucigalpa to the highest in Guatemala City. Some detailed statistics for the town center in San Salvador are available:

Public Parking		
Street Parking	Parking meters	627
	Non-metered	1,566
Off Street	Municipally owned	450
	Privately owned	833
Private Parking Lots		469

It will be observed that in San Salvador, where one would expect that the off-street fraction is probably higher than all other cities in the region, about 55 percent of parking lots are on-street. In Tegucigalpa the on-street percentage is probably near 90.

One of the striking features of parking arrangements in the area is that the

---

[6] In San Salvador the convention is to give the money to the meter-minder rather than putting it in the meter slot.

[7] A dramatic illustration of this is in Tegucigalpa. When the mission visited there in August 1967 there was only one parking lot in the town center. In January 1968 there were four—about tripling the capacity. The cost of the first hour is 16.5 cents.

parking lots are "always full."[8] This suggests that the facilities, in general, have charges which are too low. Demand exceeds supply at 5 or 10 cents an hour.[9] The fact that all parking lots are full means that a motorist cannot find a parking place at almost any price. In practice the low price of parking gives rise to queuing and even worse forms of congestion as vehicles circulate vainly seeking a place and as the motorist, in desperation, parks illegally.

Parking meters. Parking fees are collected with the help of parking meters in Guatemala City and San Salvador. No fees for on-street parking are levied in Tegucigalpa, Managua and San Jose. In Guatemala City about 4500 parking meters which roughly cover the central area of the city (18 blocks by 10 blocks) are in operation. The charges amount to 10 cents per hour in the inner zone and 5 cents per hour in the outer zone. Privately owned lots in this same area charge 25 cents for the first hour and 10 cents for each additional hour. The public parking meter system totaled gross revenues of $196,000 in 1966, of which $126,000 were used to cover administrative costs.[10] Parking regulations are strictly enforced, and incorrectly parked vehicles are towed away. The City of San Salvador operates four parking lots with a total capacity of about 1000 cars plus about 800 parking meters. In addition there are several private parking lots (total capacity: 1000 vehicles). Public parking lots and parking meters charge 6 cents per hour compared to 10 cents on the private lots. Gross revenues from parking meters can be estimated at about $60,000 per year,[11] but no data on administrative costs are available.[12]

The Use of Urban Streets

Public transport: bus services

Passenger carriage by bus (and even occasionally by truck) is important in the urban areas of all Central America. Estimates of the fraction of trips made by bus vary between 60 percent and 80 percent.[13] The explanation for the high

---

[8] This is the description given by the authorities. The observations of the mission did not discredit this account—but of course there was no opportunity to carry out an extensive survey.

[9] The exception is in Guatemala where the authorities have put parking lots in suburban areas. Of course few people ever use those when there is a nearby free curbside parking.

[10] This cost does not include the rent of the land.

[11] Gross revenue per meter/day, 24¢ assuming 300 days.

[12] The existing legal code makes enforcement difficult, but steps are being taken to correct this.

[13] For San Salvador, see *Technical Report* (Transportation Study), Adley Associates, 1968, p. 65. The figure of 60 percent for Tegucigalpa is impressionistic.

incidence of bus travel is explained by the frequency and variety of service and the low fares.

Intra-Urban Bus Fares (US cents)

Guatemala	5 (10¢ after 9 p.m.)
Honduras	There is no standard fare for Tegucigalpa
El Salvador	4
Nicaragua	4.3
Costa Rica	(2)

There is no nationalized or municipal bus service in any of the cities. Buses are operated by private firms either under conditions of free entry or on some sort of concession arrangement. In San Salvador, for example, the operating contract for a route specifies the frequency of service, the fare, the number of buses, etc. In principle it seems that entry is tightly controlled by administrative criteria; in practice, however, the controls of the central government are much loosened by informal arrangements between the parties.[14] No control is exercised over the profits of the bus firms, but if a firm is earning enough profits on its routes it appears that new franchises are issued to other firms. A somewhat similar method of control is used in Guatemala through the municipality and Department of Public Works; however, the existing bus operators have formed a cartel and divided up the city, and it is difficult for a new operator to obtain a concession. One may conjecture that this accounts for the somewhat higher fares in Guatemala, but many other factors might also explain the difference. In San Jose, Costa Rica, the situation is similar to San Salvador. The franchise is issued on the criteria of technical competence, financial stability and so on. Charges are made for changes of schedules and extension of lines and the cost varies between 100 and 500 colones (US$13–65). The concessions are for 10 years and may be sold on paying an ad valorem tax of 0.4 percent.[15] Usually a route is the monopoly of one bus operator, but occasionally two operators will exist side by side on a route. The authority, Direcciones de Transportes, decides on the routes (perhaps from suggestions from existing operators or from the public) and puts the concession out to tender. The price or fare is, however, not open to tender—the authority has a fixed scale or fares—and the criterion for choosing between the tenders is the "quality of the service." This includes a wide variety of considerations such as frequency, type of equipment, etc. The existing bus

---

[14] The average size of bus firm is small. There are 495 buses in San Salvador and the largest operator has less than 80.

[15] The price of these franchises can reach as much as 100,000 colones (US$ 13,000).

owners are, however, given preference over newcomers. The fares for bus services vary according to distance, but they can be as low as 2 US cents.

In Managua the picture is again similar to that of San Salvador and San Jose. Proposals for new services normally come from existing operators, and they are given preference by the Ministry of Economy's Council. Again the criteria are the adequacy of facilities, quality of service, etc.; the fare is fixed at 0.30 cordobas (4.3 US cents). This is too low for certain types of services involving relatively long distances, and consequently these are not offered by the operators. An attempt by bus operators and the Ministry to raise the standard fare for all routes met much local opposition and the proposal was dropped. It is alleged that bus owners make very low profits and that there is too much competition.[16] There is no concrete evidence of either of these allegations, however.

Although there are a few standard size buses in Tegucigalpa, the predominant mode of conveyance is the mini-bus carrying 16 to 20 passengers. The reason for the ubiquity of the mini-bus is the narrowness of the city streets; full-size buses find it very difficult to negotiate the city center. There is no regulation of bus services in Tegucigalpa. Equipment, services, routes, frequencies and fares have adapted to the demands of the traveling public. The small bus owner-driver is the predominant firm. Fares are low and the service seems to be efficient.

The main conclusion to be drawn from this survey of bus transport in the area is that competition, although somewhat muted by government and political interference, does provide cheap and frequent service. The organization of the small firms permits close supervision by the proprietor, enabling him to keep down costs and respond with alacrity to the demands of the traveling public. It also provides a valuable outlet for entrepreneurial talent and, correspondingly, an on-the-job training in entrepreneurial skills. Minor improvements in government supervision could be made to permit more competitiveness and freedom of entry, and perhaps more systematic inspection of safety conditions. At present the preoccupation of many of the bus regulatory agencies is to expand the scope of their activities. There is in fact a danger that excessive resort to regulation will impede the development of bus transportation.

There are, however, many problems of congestion caused by present bus services.[17] Much of the congestion could be avoided if bus stops were regulated (or if existing controls were enforced) and if routes were reorganized. Later

---

[16] In Managua operators are predominantly small-scale—the average size of fleet is in the vicinity of 5 vehicles.

[17] Although it is important to stress that the same number of passengers carried by cars—or even by bicycles—would generate much more congestion.

in this chapter the possibility of arranging user charges to encourage a more efficient use of the city streets by bus services is explored.

Public transport: taxi services

Taxis provide the most important competition to the bus. The ubiquity of the taxi in the capital cities of Central America (in marked contrast to most cities in the industrialized world) is explained partly by the low incidence of car ownership, but perhaps mainly by the low fares. There is considerable variation in the fare according to distance, origin and destination, the type of vehicle, and the number of passengers. A few typical fares are:

Managua (anywhere in town)	1 cordoba (14 cents) *per person*
San Jose	2 colones (24 cents) 1st km *per vehicle* + 1 colon (12 cents) a km *per vehicle*
Tegucigalpa (anywhere in town)	30 cents (15 cents) *per person*
San Salvador	2.00–2.5 colones (80 cents to $1.)
Guatemala	1 quetzal ($1.) for 3.5 km *per vehicle*

Note: The rates in San Salvador and Guatemala are relatively high but are open to some bargaining so that the actual rate may well be much below these levels. Values in parentheses are US$ equivalents.

Although taxi fares are regulated in certain cities (such as San Jose), the authorities have not in fact enforced the laws. Fares are settled by competition, so that for similar journeys one price emerges on the market. In certain cases "rings" have been effective in keeping up the price, but these seem to be of minor importance.[18] The pressure of competition exerts its own discipline.

Economic regulations governing taxis generally either do not exist or are ineffective. Entry into the industry is all but free in most of the countries; the exception is in San Jose where there are a fixed number of taxis but a taxi license may be purchased for about 5,000 colones (US$680) from an existing franchise holder. Normally, however, the fee for a taxi license is not sufficiently high to effectively discourage entry. All types of vehicles from the very small to the very large may be employed, and no country employs taxi meters; essentially any car can be converted into a taxi at little or no cost.

Yet another reason for the low fares—particularly in Managua—is the system of shared taxis. Shared taxis greatly increase the utilization of the

---

[18] The most common example of this occurs in travel from the airports.

vehicle and thus reduce the money cost of a passenger trip. Typically the passenger to seat ratio of taxis seems to be much higher in Central America than in the cities of the United States and Europe, although there is no statistical evidence to support this conjecture.

The general conclusion is, therefore, that taxi services in the area are broadly organized and effectively run. Taxi services have responded well to the needs of the public, and journeys are supplied at relatively low fares. Minor improvements could be effected by removing some of the existing political and administrative interference with freedom of entry. Competition will ensure that fares are low and that the supply of services responds to new economic, social and technological conditions. It would be unwise to encourage the governments to introduce any system of regulated taxis with restricted entry such as that which exists in European and North American cities.[19] On the other hand, it is clear that the more efficient use of the city streets does require the enforcement of limited stopping and pick-up points. Improved vehicle maintenance and a high standard of driver behavior are desirable, but the economic structure of taxi business leaves little to be desired.

Private use of urban streets

The most predominant use of urban streets is by private passenger vehicles. The following figures are averages for San Jose (the only city for which such data are available), but spot checks by the mission in other cities indicate that they are typical for all major cities of Central America.

	Percentage of Vehicle Flow
Light Vehicles (passenger and pickups)	92
Buses	6
Cargo Vehicles	2
	100

In contrast, the percentage of heavy vehicles on interurban highways is much higher—from 35 percent to 55 percent.

While some of the light vehicles using city streets are commercial vehicles (taxis and delivery trucks), a large percentage are private vehicles. A survey in San Salvador indicates that 80 percent of vehicles registered in the San Salvador area make on the average two trips into and out of the central business district everyday.[20] Non-motor vehicle use of urban streets is not sig-

---

[19] Some observers state that the taxi owners are not making sufficient profit to maintain suitable services. The evidence available seemed to indicate, however, a growing and profitable business rather than a bankrupt or dying service.

[20] Adley Associates, *Transportation Study.*

115

nificant in Central America. Animal-drawn carts are found only occasionally on city streets. In some areas (as around market places), pedestrians spill over into the street causing delays to vehicle traffic.

Congestion Costs

Evidence of congestion

In the analysis and formulation of policy for road user charges one of the critical features is the incidence of congestion. The statistics available on average trip times or journey speeds in urban areas indicate the existence of severe congestion in all the metropolitan areas in Central America. A recent study of San Jose (Costa Rica) shows that the average speed in the city (excluding the outskirts) during the day is approximately 15 km/hr.[21] During the rush hour the speed falls to 4–10 km/hr. In Tegucigalpa the study team collected data on journey speeds at various times of the day for various typical trips. These trips included a high fraction of suburban travel, but nevertheless the average overall journey speed was between 10 and 12 km an hour. In the central area of Tegucigalpa the speeds were very low indeed—falling to less than 4 km an hour over a measured kilometer during the rush hour. Traffic was often in a complete jam for several minutes during the peak periods.[22]

In the larger cities or conurbations in the region—Guatemala City, San Salvador and Managua—similar levels of congestion were also observed. The more extensive modern suburban development and the provision of motor roads in the suburbs has produced a contrast between suburban and city motoring. While the suburbs on the outskirts are not without congestion, average speeds for journeys confined to the suburbs are normally between 20 and 35 km an hour. The ordinary city traffic experiences journey speeds typical of those in San Jose and Tegucigalpa. The narrow streets combined with the high density of traffic give speeds of 5 to 15 km an hour with occasionally complete stoppage for several minutes. Owing to the higher fraction of suburban running, the journey speed for the average trip is probably somewhat higher in the large cities than in, say, Tegucigalpa. But it must also be true that the average trip length is probably higher.

Much of the congestion and traffic chaos in urban areas is a consequence of the pattern of city streets. Generally the cities were laid out in the pre-motor age and little adaptation has taken place to accommodate the auto-

---

[21] Ministry of Transport, 1965 and 1966.
[22] This occurred not only at the usual morning and early evening hours, but also at mid-day.

mobile. This is, of course, an endemic problem of all cities, except the newer ones such as San Pedro Sula. To rebuild and remodel cities is usually prohibitively expensive, however. For this reason it is probably more realistic to assume that policy must be framed within the context of existing cities.

Estimating the costs. The estimates of the costs of congestion proceed in several stages. First it is necessary to examine the relationship between speed and flow, and once this has been established to examine the effect of speed on costs. Once the costs have been estimated it is then possible, given certain assumptions about the demand for urban streets, to estimate the costs to the economy of not rationing the use of urban streets through the price system.

The speed-volume relationship

There are two basic forms for the speed-flow relationship. First there is an approximately linear negative relationship between speed and vehicle flow for traffic conditions that are not severely congested. When traffic density is high, however, the flow may actually be decreased as the speed is reduced. The increase in the number of vehicles attempting to use the over-crowded highway increases the density of traffic; thus speed is reduced to the point where the actual flow is also reduced. The flow of vehicles per hour is equal to the density (vehicles per kilometer) times the speed. These conditions are shown in Figure 4. The curve is approximately flat from S to A—the uncongested traffic volumes. The AB situation is where the speed and flow are (approximately) related by a line with negative slope. The BMD situation is one

FIGURE 4
THE SPEED-FLOW RELATIONSHIP

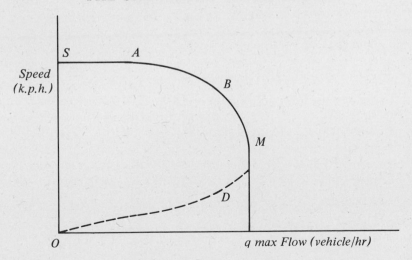

where the flow continues increasing to M; although density increases, the flow goes on increasing in spite of the drop in speed. After M—where traffic flow is at a maximum, q max—the effect of the increase in density on speed is so marked that the flow is actually reduced; this is the experience of the MD part of the curve. In principle the curve can be thought of as going back to the origin (shown in the figure as a broken line from D to O); this shows the "complete jam" at zero speed and flow associated with bumper-to-bumper density. Of course it must be remembered that in principle this curve applies to speed-flow characteristics in a short period. One can in practice observe such a pattern as BMD for ten minute intervals. For large periods such as an hour one observes only the AB or perhaps the ABM relationship with a scatter of points at the high-flow end of the curve.

The speed-flow characteristics of traffic may be broadly characterized as where:

SA represents uncongested interurban roads with traffic densities less than 100 vehicles an hour.

AB represents congested interurban highways or even restricted access highways in suburban areas.

BMD represents the congested city streets.

The constants vary according to the width of the highways, the number of intersections, the types of traffic control, the incidence of pedestrian crossings, etc. Information on these constants is available for countries such as the United States and Great Britain. Evidence on these speed-flow relationships in Central America is, however, scant and flimsy. What must be done is to use the data available on Central America in the context of general knowledge from other countries in order to make some estimate as to the form which the curve will take.

The AB part of the curve—typical of the free flowing arteries of suburban areas—has been measured in the San Jose areas in Costa Rica.[23] Speed-volume relationships are found for the following roads:

Tramo Primer Amor—Pirro   Speed = $52 - 0.019$ (veh/hr) (km/hr)

Tramo San Pedro—Curridabat   Speed = $54 - 0.0029$ (veh/hr) (km/hr)

Tramo Curridabat—Tres Rios   Speed = $54 - 0.022$ (veh/hr) (km/hr)

These roads leading out of San Jose are partly of a suburban free-running type

---

[23] *Estudio de Velocidades en las Carreteras de Costa Rica, San Jose*, 1964, p. 46.

and partly of the interurban kind. Vehicle flows over the 12-hour day vary between 80 and 330 an hour. The roads are two-lane asphalt highways (width of pavement 6.1 to 6.25 meters) traversing hilly terrain.

These results may be compared with the typical results for roads in the United Kingdom.[24] Speeds are as follows:

$$\text{Urban (30 feet wide)} \quad \text{Speed} = 40 - 0.023 \text{ (veh/hr)}$$
$$\text{(km/hr)}$$

$$\text{Rural (3 lane)} \quad \text{Speed} = 77 - 0.010 \text{ (veh/hr)}$$
$$\text{(km/hr)}$$

(Vehicles are here enumerated in passenger car units or PCU's.) The free-running speeds on urban highways (40) and on rural highways (77) straddle those of the San Jose results. The coefficients describing the reduction in speed of San Jose traffic due to an extra vehicle an hour are (0.019 to 0.029), roughly the same as in the urban areas of the United Kingdom (0.023). Broadly speaking the results for San Jose suburbs are consistent with those for the United Kingdom.

Direct observations suggest that there are no marked differences in suburban traffic conditions in Guatemala City, San Salvador, Managua and San Jose. Unfortunately no statistical evidence on speed-volume relationships (other than those in San Jose suburbs) is available to check these conjectures.[25] Since the journey speeds are similar, however, the speed-volume relationships are also likely to be approximately the same.

The central areas of large towns in the region are as crowded as the most congested districts to be found in other cities of the world. Vehicle speeds are, for example, below those of Central London and New York. One would suspect, therefore, that a speed-volume relationship such as *BMD* (in Figure 4) would emerge from the data. Unfortunately no detailed statistics are available for sufficiently short periods (such as 10, 15 and 20 minutes) to check this hypothesis. Again the only reliable data are for San Jose (Costa Rica) and usually these have been aggregated over the day so that the figures are for daily traffic flow and average speed during the day on different stretches of urban roads.[26] The data are, therefore, a cross section of road segments rather than observations at different times on the same part of the road.

[24] *Research on Road Traffic, HMSO* (London, 1965).

[25] The absence of speed-volume statistics in Central America (with the exception of Costa Rica) is one of the most glaring inadequacies of road statistics. They could easily be supplied and at a very low cost.

[26] One would normally prefer to have the separate hourly traffic flows and associated speeds. But the extent of the diurnal variation in San Jose as in San Salvador is surprisingly small (see *Estudio de Velocidades en las Carreteras de Costa Rica* (1964), pp. 61–62).

119

The data on speed and flow has been plotted for Avenida 1 in San Jose—the main artery of the town. (This stretch of the road is used as an example as it has constant width and about the same incidence of controlled intersections throughout). The speed-volume relationship revealed by the data is of no neat form such as there is in Figure 4 above.[27] This is to be expected since there is obviously considerable heterogeneity in the road segments in, for example, illegal and legal parking and stopping. The speed or flow conditions may be determined by conditions in adjacent segments, the inflow and outflow; furthermore, the aggregate obscures much of the interesting information. Nevertheless, it can be adduced that the road is very congested. The density on this single-lane avenue must exceed 100 vehicles a kilometer for the peak periods.[28] The speeds are also very low (on the average in the region of 10 km/hr), and it must be recalled that this is the average for a day. The scatter suggests that the maximum daily flow for a given hourly distribution is about 6,000 vehicles.

The high density, the low speeds and the fact that for some low-speed segments the flow is actually less than the maximum are all evidence suggesting this street of San Jose experiences traffic conditions over the *BMD* range of Figure 4 above. Additional evidence on this point can be adduced from hourly tabulations of traffic flow and speed on four streets in San Jose. Unfortunately, owing to the lack of simultaneity of speed and volume observations, one cannot expect to observe a *BMD* curve. Indeed one important feature of San Jose traffic particularly inhibits the emergence of such a curve; there is relatively little diurnal variation in traffic flow. It is remarkable that for some periods the speed is much higher than others—whereas the flow does not vary very much—about 400 to 600 vehicles an hour. This basic pattern appears in all the other speed-volume statistics, not merely for the Avenida Central but also for the other four streets used in this sample. There was little variation in traffic flow although there were considerable differences in speeds.

This evidence is consistent with the proposition that the main variation in the streets of San Jose is the traffic density not the flow. Congestion is so severe that during peak hours the flow is reduced to little more than the off-peak period by the great density of traffic and the snail-like pace. Evidence to support this view can be adduced from the diurnal flow statistics. There is in fact very little "peakiness" in the flow of traffic compared with cities in the United States and Europe. The demand for road space fills the gaps left during the

---

[27] See Figure 5 for speed-volume relation at different times of the day.

[28] These data were especially prepared by the Mission; nevertheless flow and velocity statistics for the same period could not be obtained. There is, therefore, much "noise" in the scatter.

day—albeit at higher speeds in view of the lower density. Congestion is not merely "a matter of an hour or so" during the four peak periods; it lasts the whole day long.[29]

Much less data are available for the other cities in the region. No speed-volume relationship can be adduced, but what evidence is available does suggest that somewhat similar conditions apply in all other cities. A survey of San Salvador, for example, showed that in 1967 there were flows of a magnitude similar to those of San Jose. More remarkably there was an even smaller diurnal variation. One may conjecture that in the city center the experience was similar: an increase in density at so-called peak periods and a slowing-up of traffic so that flow is not very different from volume during off-peak (day) hours.

Some journey speeds were measured in other cities, but since no corresponding flow data were collected it is not possible to test the contention that congestion primarily appears in the density rather than in the flow. The speed results are summarized below.

Typical Journey Speeds

	Day (km/hr)	Peak (km/hr)
Costa Rica (San Jose)[a]	15	4–10
Nicaragua (Managua)[b]	14–20	6–10
Honduras (Tegucigalpa)[c]	10–12	4–6
Guatemala (City)[d]	15–28	

[a] Averages for central districts
[b] Overall journey speeds in central areas.
[c] Overall journey speeds for "normal" mission journeys in city.
[d] Includes a high fraction of suburban traffic conditions.

Only the very broad orders of magnitude of these results should be taken into account, for with the exception of San Jose the sampling basis of the figures is very slender. Nevertheless, from these general observations in the cities and from this data it can be adduced that conditions are broadly similar.

Again it is useful to compare these results for Costa Rica with those of developed countries. One might first attempt to locate the speed at maximum

---

[29] It is interesting to observe that these statistics are also consistent with the data on suburban traffic where there was only a very small peak in the traffic flow.

flow (i.e., the speed associated with the point M in Figure 4.) For urban streets there are several observations that suggest that the average trip speed is about 8 mph or 13 km/hr for the maximum capacity.[30] It seems likely, however, that the flow does not change very much for trip speeds between 6 to 9 mph (or 9.6 to 14.4 km/hr) since the curve turns around gently and not sharply at M. These are broadly the same as the average speeds in the central area of San Jose. This suggests therefore, that for certain hours of the day the density of traffic was so great that the flow falls below the maximum and speed falls below 10 kph.

Further analysis of congestion[31]

For congested traffic there is much evidence that the speed is determined by the density of vehicles.[32] The observed relationship between speed and density is similar to that of the function connecting velocity and density of a uni-dimensional fluid flow. Elementary theory of fluid dynamics shows that:

$$s = B \log \frac{D_0}{D}$$

where s = speed of fluid flow

D = density of fluid

D_0 = density of fluid when the speed falls to zero (the traffic jam)

B = positive constant (in units of distance per unit time) which depends on "width of pipe" and friction. For natural logarithms, it is the speed obtained when density is .4343 of the jam density D_0.

It is easy to translate the fluid dynamics into a vehicle traffic flow where s is the speed of the traffic stream, D the density of vehicles in terms of number of vehicles per kilometer, while D_0 is the bumper-to-bumper density of the

---

[30] See C. A. Rothrock and L. E. Keefer "Traffic Speeds and Volume Measurement" *Highway Research Board Bulletin* 156, pp. 1–13 (1956). A. A. Walters "The Theory and Measurement of Private and Social Costs of Highway Congestion" *Econometrica,* 1961, pp. 676–99. The Road Research Laboratory suggests that the present journey speed of 8.6 mph is a little more than the speed at which capacity is maximized. See *Road Research, 1964,* pp. 28–30.

[31] This section discusses the derivation of the elasticity of speed with respect to flow. It is somewhat complicated and may be omitted without losing the continuity of the argument.

[32] See, for example, Greenberg, "An Analysis of Traffic Flow" *Operations Research,* 1959, and A. C. Dick, "Speed-flow Relationship Within an Urban Area," *Traffic Engineering and Control,* October 1960.

FIGURE 5
THE SPEED-DENSITY RELATIONSHIP

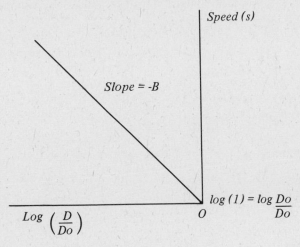

complete jam. Density increases as the speed falls until at zero speed the density is at a maximum. (See Figure 5.)

This speed-density relationship can be translated into a speed-flow relationship by means of the following identity.

$$q = sD$$

where q is the vehicle flow per unit time. The speed-density relationship can be solved for D, giving

$$D = D_0 \, e^{-s/B}$$

so that

$$q = D_0 \, s \, e^{-s/B}.$$

To find the speed for which flow is a maximum, this can be differentiated with respect to s, and the result set equal to zero, giving

$$\frac{dq}{ds} = D_0 \, e^{-s/B} \left(1 - \frac{s}{B} \right) = 0,$$

which gives $s = B$ as the speed for which flow is a maximum, so that we can write $B = s_m$. For $s = s_m = B$, we have $D_m = D_0 \, e^{-1}$ and $q_m = D_0 \, s_m \, e^{-1}$; thus the maximum flow occurs for a density $\frac{1}{e} = 0.368$ times the jam density, and

$$q = q_m \, e \left(\frac{s}{s_m} \right) e^{-s/s_m} = q_m \, \frac{s}{s_m} \, e^{1-s/s_m}.$$

123

The average time required for each vehicle to go a unit distance is $t = \dfrac{1}{s}$, and the total time spent in going a unit distance by the vehicles passing a given point in a unit time is $T = qt = \dfrac{q_m}{s_m} e^{1-s/s_m} = D_m e^{(1-s/s_m)}$.

The marginal cost, in terms of total time, of adding a unit of traffic to the stream is then

$$M = \frac{dT}{dq} = \frac{dT}{ds}\frac{ds}{dq} = \frac{\dfrac{dT}{ds}}{\dfrac{dq}{ds}} = \frac{-D_m(1/s_m)\,e^{(1-s/s_m)}}{D_0(1 - s/s_m)\,e^{-s/s_m}} = \frac{1}{s - s_m}.$$

Of this total marginal cost, an amount $t = \dfrac{1}{s}$ is borne by the operator of each vehicle, so that the amount of delay his addition to the traffic stream causes to others will be given by

$$Z = M - t = \frac{1}{s - s_m} - \frac{1}{s} = \frac{s_m}{s(s - s_m)} = t\,\frac{s_m}{s - s_m}.$$

Accordingly, if traffic is flowing at twice the maximum flow speed, s_m, each vehicle is increasing the delay to others by an amount equal to the time he himself spends on the road; while if the speed is only 20 percent above the maximum flow speed the delay imposed is equal to five times the time the particular vehicle spends traveling under such conditions.

For a roadway with a maximum flow (q_m) of 1000 vehicles per hour at a speed (s_m) of 9 km/hr, the results can be set forth in Table 7.3.

The calculations for Table 7.3 can be carried out as follows: Let $\mathcal{Q}_0$ be the current volume of traffic, moving at a speed $s_0 = \dfrac{3600}{t_0}$ and let k be the elasticity of the demand curve. Then the demand curve can be written $\mathcal{Q} = \mathcal{Q}_0 \left(\dfrac{p}{t_0 + a}\right)^{-k}$ where a is the time equivalent of the non-time costs, and p is the total cost of the user expressed in time units. The marginal cost curve is given by $M = \dfrac{3600}{s - p} + a$, where s is the speed in km per hour, a is as above, and M, a, t_0, and p are expressed in seconds. The relation between s and $\mathcal{Q}$ given by the fluid dynamics model is $\mathcal{Q} = \mathcal{Q}_m \dfrac{s}{s_m} e^{-s/s_m}$. Putting $y = s/s_m$ and equating $MC = p$ to obtain the optimum point on the demand curve, and noting that if the original point is a point on the average cost curve, $\mathcal{Q}_0 = \mathcal{Q}_m y_0 e^{-y_0}$, we have

$$\mathcal{Q} = \mathcal{Q}_m y\, e^{-y} = \mathcal{Q}_m y_0\, e^{-y_0} \left(\frac{M}{t_0 + a}\right)^{-k}$$

124

TABLE 7.3: Flows and Costs for Various Speeds

Speed km/hr S	Relative Density $D_0 = 1.00$ D	Relative Flow $\mathcal{Q}_{max} = 1.0$ $\mathcal{Q}$	Average Time secs/km t	Total Time vehicle/secs km $\mathcal{Q}t$	Marginal Time secs/km $M = \dfrac{d(\mathcal{Q}t)}{d\mathcal{Q}}$	Externality Time secs/km $X = M - t$
1	.894	.2702	3600	972.7		
2	.801	.4836	1800	870.5		
3	.717	.6492	1200	779.0		
4	.641	.7746	900	697.1		
5	.574	.8664	720	623.8		
6	.513	.9304	600	558.2		
7	.459	.9713	514	499.5		
8	.411	.9933	450	447.0		
8.5	.389	.9984	424	422.8		
9	.368	1.0000	400	400.0		
9.1	.363	0.9999	396	395.5	36,000	35,604
9.2	.360	0.9998	391	391.2	18,000	17,609
9.3	.356	.9994	387	386.9	12,000	11,613
9.5	.348	.9985	379	378.4	7,200	6,822
9.7	.340	.9971	371	370.0	5,143	4,872
10.0	.329	.9943	360	357.9	3,600	3,240
10.5	.311	.9876	343	338.5	2,400	2,057
11	.295	.9787	327	320.3	1,800	1,473
12	.264	.9554	300	286.6	1,200	900
13	.236	.9261	277	258.9	900	623
14	.211	.8925	257	229.5	720	463
15	,189	.8557	240	205.4	600	360
17	.151	.7765	212	164.4	450	238
20	.108	,6546	180	117.8	327	147
25	.062	.4695	144	67.6	225	81

or
$$y\, e^{-y}\, M^k = y\, e^{-y}\left(\frac{400}{y-1} + a\right)^k = y_0\, e^{-y_0}\left(\frac{3600}{s_0} + a\right)^k$$

Taking Logarithms, we get

$$\log y - y + k \log\left(\frac{1}{y-1} + \frac{a}{400}\right) = \log y_0 - y_0 + k \log\left(\frac{1}{y} + \frac{a}{400}\right)$$

and the right hand side of this expression can first be evaluated and the left hand side solved by successive approximations for the corresponding value of y, from which the corresponding s, $\mathcal{Q}$, M, and the optimal toll can be derived. The net gain can be calculated by deducting the change in total cost from the change in total benefits, the latter being represented by the area under the demand curve, obtained by integrating $p\, dq = (t_0 + a)$ $(\mathcal{Q}/\mathcal{Q}_0)^{-k}$ over the range $\mathcal{Q}$ to $\mathcal{Q}_0$, getting $(t_0 + a)\mathcal{Q}_0(1 - (\mathcal{Q}/\mathcal{Q}_0^{-k})$. The change in total cost, which corresponds to the area under the marginal cost curve,

is simply $(t_0 + a)\mathcal{Q}_0 - (t + a)\mathcal{Q}$, so that the net gain can be computed as
$$(t_0 + a)\,\mathcal{Q}_0(\mathcal{Q}/\mathcal{Q}_0)^{-k} = (t + a)\mathcal{Q} = p_0\mathcal{Q}_0\left(\frac{p}{p_0} - \frac{p\mathcal{Q}}{p_0\mathcal{Q}_0}\right).$$

For speeds below $s_m = 9$ km/hr, marginal cost and externality cost have no direct meaning: under these conditions the attempt of another vehicle to joint the flow will actually result in fewer vehicle succeeding in getting through within a given time, with the result that traffic will tend to accumulate until either some would-be travelers are turned away by the increased delay, or the delay shifts some of the traffic to an off-peak period when it can be gradually worked off. The costs under these conditions can be very high in terms of waiting time or in trips forgone, but cannot be represented in terms of a speed-flow relationship. In any case such speeds represent an inherently inefficient situation in which adequate control, whether by user charges or otherwise, can always be made to result in both greater traffic flow and higher speeds, even though in many cases an even better result would be somewhat reduced flow and even higher speeds.

Cost and speed

In order to transform the speed-flow relationship into cost-flow functions, it is necessary to find a function relating cost to speed. Cost before tax is defined as the money payments made, or the physical depreciation for the kilometer of the vehicle journey. One problem is to find a valuation for the non-working time of drivers and their passengers. In principle the amount which people actually pay in order to save an hour spent in traffic should be measured.[33] No data are available for a direct estimate of this valuation, but certain indirect estimates can be easily incorporated. The basic equation relating cost and speed is:

$$c = 2.8 + 93/s$$

for speeds up to about 60 kph, on paved highways where c is the cost in US cents per equivalent car per kilometer net of tax, and s is the velocity or speed in kilometers per hour. No value is assigned in this equation to non-working time. If non-working time were to be given a value, an adjustment must be made in the last term. The average hourly wage in Costa Rican industry is about 50 US cents an hour, and probably the average occupancy of cars is around two. Recalling that the average hourly earnings of car travellers is likely to be higher than the average—say 80 to 100 cents—and taking 50 per-

---

[33] For the basic data behind these figures see J. A. Bruce and J. O. Fressider, "Characteristics of Rural Roads in Jamaica," Conference on Civil Engineering Problems Overseas. Technical Session IV, June 15, 1966, p. 35.

cent as the appropriate valuation factor for non-working time, the last term of the cost speed relationship would be between the limits $173/s$ and $193/s$. The cost speed relationship may be taken as roughly:

$$c = 2.8 + 183/s \qquad s < 60$$

There is probably some variation in the cost-velocity relationship from one country to another, but such variations are likely to be small enough to be encompassed in the error in this equation.[34]

As can be seen, when speeds are very low the variation in cost is almost inversely proportional to the speed. The second term $(93/s)$ is very large compared with the first term (2.8). But for higher speeds of $(34$ kph and over) the constant term 2.8 is the dominant element of cost.

In the analysis that follows the value of non-working time has normally been taken at zero. This convention biases downward all the estimates of congestion costs. The reason for this approach is that it is difficult to obtain any agreement on the appropriate valuation of non-working time. The fraction of 50 percent of the value of working time, although based on solid data, is probably not entirely relevant for a developing country. On the other hand the convention of valuing non-working time at zero is clearly wrong; it must be worth something. In the following pages the congestion costs have been normally calculated for the case where no value has been attached to leisure time. But in order to indicate the effects of this assumption (and bias), the values of certain coefficients have been recalculated using $183/s$ as the variable cost instead of $93/s$. These values have an asterisk associated with them, and the reader can then examine some of the effects of this assumption.

Cost of congestion

The cost of congestion can be calculated by putting together the cost-velocity function and the speed-flow relationship. An immediate difficulty is that with the speed-flow relationships of San José, the density during the peak is that of the "backward-bending" part of the curve. A reduction in density would achieve an increase in speed giving roughly the same or even an increased flow. In principle, congestion charges should be such that these conditions do not occur with any regularity. In the calculation of congestion costs at the margin, however, only the *off-peak* traffic or traffic on the negatively sloped part of the speed-flow curve will be considered. This, of course, will underestimate the costs of congestion.

---

[34] One should not be surprised to find that this function is close to that adduced for Britain. One can expect that in Costa Rica the income level at which car ownership takes place is broadly the same as that in Europe especially since the cost of motoring is not so very different.

Taking first the outlying suburban traffic between satellite towns and San Jose, the speed-volume relationship can be approximated by:[35]

$$\text{Speed} = 53 - 0.023 \,(\text{veh/hr})$$
$$(\text{kph})$$

The cost relationship (excluding drivers time) is roughly:

$$\text{Average Cost} = 2.8 + \frac{93}{(\text{speed})}$$
(US cents per veh/km)

Substituting:

$$\text{Average Cost} = 2.8 + \frac{93}{53 - 0.012 \,(\text{veh/hr})}$$
(cents per veh/km)

It is easy to see, however, that the maintenance of speeds above 45 kph which occurs for flows less than 346 veh/hr, does make the marginal congestion cost quite small for traffic between the satellite towns and San Jose. From the calculations it can be seen that it is of trivial importance for cars and certainly less than 0.5 US cents a kilometer for even the large trucks and trailers. This suggests that it can easily be incorporated in, for example, a gasoline (or more generally a fuel) duty; this problem is discussed below.

The second case to consider is that of heavily congested city traffic. The relationships between speed, density, flow and time developed from the fluid-dynamic model of congested traffic, can readily be used to develop corresponding cost relationships simply by converting the time costs of congestion into money cost by means of the appropriate value of time. The relationship $c = 2.8 + 93/s$ implies a value of time of 93¢/hr, or 1.55¢/minute or .0258¢/sec, and similarly the relationship $c = 2.8 + 183/s$ implies $1.83/hr, 3.05¢/ minute or .0583¢/sec. One can then simply multiply the time costs by the appropriate factor and add the constant term of 2.8¢ to get the total costs. It is for some purposes more convenient, however, to convert the constant 2.8¢/km into an equivalent in terms of time, and add this to the total time costs to get a total cost in terms of time equivalent, which can then be converted back into money terms at the appropriate rate. If this is done we can draw the curves for average and marginal congestion cost in terms of time as shown in Figure 6; we then add two additional scales on the vertical axis in terms of which these curves can be read in terms of cents per veh/km. Any

---

[35] *Estudio de Velocidades*, pp. 61–62.

FIGURE 6
AVERAGE AND MARGINAL CONGESTION COSTS

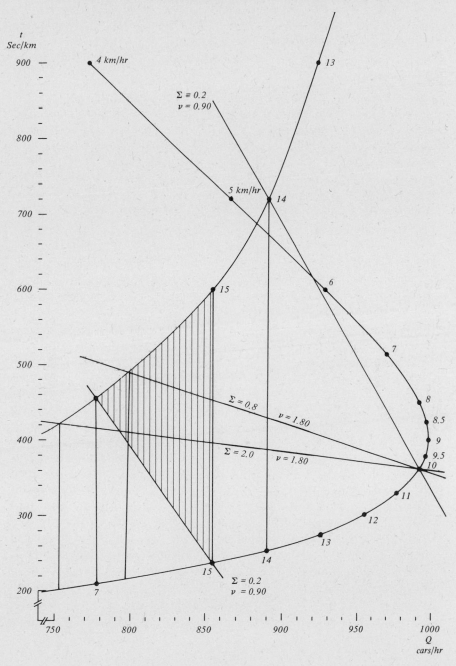

given speed will imply a corresponding average time per km, and the corresponding flow can be read from the diagram by reference to the average cost curve. For speeds above the maximum flow speed, giving average times below that for maximum flow, one can also obtain for the corresponding flow the corresponding marginal and externality costs.

Demand conditions

It is important to emphasize that these are congestion costs at certain specified speeds. Thus 9 cents a kilometer, for example, measures the excess of marginal cost over private cost at 15 kph. The optimum congestion levies that should be raised would be somewhat less than these values calculated on the basis of existing speeds, because they would have to take into account the reduction in traffic flow due to the increased price, and so the increase in speed. The increase in velocity would reduce private cost and the elasticity of cost with respect to traffic volume. The condition of equilibrium for the optimum tax is then given by:

$$\text{private cost} + \text{congestion levy} = \text{price} = \emptyset\ (x),$$

where $\emptyset\ (x)$ is the price (including tax) which people would be willing to pay for x vehicle kilometers. This function describes the demand conditions in urban areas.

The only information available on the demand conditions in urban areas is the single observation of speed (cost) and traffic volume for that particular hour of the day. There has been no study of the elasticity of demand for the space on urban streets—and for reasons of identification such a study is difficult to undertake. Nevertheless it is possible to experiment with the implications of different levels of elasticity to observe what ranges of optimum toll levels and what ranges of benefits from road pricing are plausible. Table 7.4 gives a sample of such results, starting from an assumption that current speeds reflect a condition where costs borne by users reflect only average congestion costs, so that the position can be represented by a point on the average cost curve. From this point one can draw demand curves of varying elasticities and observe where they intersect the marginal cost curve to determine the optimal flow of traffic, from which the corresponding marginal cost, average cost, and user charge can be determined. For cases where the original speed was above the maximum flow speed, the net gain from the imposition of the user charge can be measured by the area between the demand curve, the marginal cost curve, and the ordinate at the original flow level. For cases where the original speed was below the maximum flow speed, one would of course choose the lower of the two average cost levels as a basis for determining the user charge.

130

In this case the net gain can be thought of as consisting of two parts, the first being the gain from carrying the same amount of traffic at the lower congestion cost represented by the lower rather than the higher branch of the average cost curve—which is the rectangle having as base the current volume of traffic and as height the difference between the average cost at this volume of traffic for the two branches of the curve. In addition to this there will be the further gain from the adjustment of the level of traffic from the existing to the optimum level, represented again by the triangle between the marginal cost, demand, and ordinate at the existing volume.

The values given in Table 7.4 are for a road with maximum flow of 1,000 vehicles per hour at 9 km/hr, but these can be adjusted for other sizes of roads and maximum flow speeds by appropriate changes in the units. It will be seen that fairly extreme assumptions as to elasticities make relatively little difference in the optimum toll, and the differences in the benefits obtainable are not such as to make the desirability of road pricing depend very sharply on the assumptions made in this respect. Far more important is the degree of congestion as reflected in the current speeds assumed, and in the value placed on the saving of time. It should also be noted that the relative loss from failure to achieve the optimum toll is approximately proportional to the square of the deviation of the toll from the optimal; so that, for example, even if the actual toll were to be as much as 40 percent short or in excess of the optimal toll, the benefits would still amount to 84 percent of the benefits attainable with the optimal toll for the less extremely congested situations and even higher proportions in the more congested situations. $(.84 = 1.00 - (.4)^2)$. Thus very rough measures can still yield substantial benefits.

Perhaps the best that can be done at this stage, given the limitations of the data, is to suggest that the congestion costs for situations where speed is now about 15 kph are somewhat less than 9 cents a kilometer and probably are within the range of 5–7 cents a kilometer. For situations where speeds are now 12 kph the range is probably 9–12 cents a kilometer. These figures are only very broad orders of magnitude, but they are good enough as a basis for formulating policy. The administrative instruments available are axes rather than scalpels and precision is not required.

As this analysis had been pursued only for San Jose, it is reasonable to inquire whether or not the same conditions are repeated in the other cities of the region. From the fragmentary data on journey speeds and from the observations of the study team it seems that San Jose is by no means unique. Tegucigalpa is perhaps more congested than San Jose, Managua about on a par, and San Salvador and Guatemala City somewhat less congested. Similarly the same characteristics of traffic flow are found, for example, in San Salvador;

TABLE 7.4: Optimum Tolls and Results for Various Initial Conditions

Initial Speed Without Toll, kph	S_0		4	6	8	10	12	15	25
Flow (Capacity = 1000)	Q_0		774.6	930.4	993.3	994.3	955.4	855.7	469.5
Average Time, Minutes	t_0		15.00	10.00	7.50	6.0	5.00	4.00	2.40
Total Time	T_0		11619	9304	7450	5965	4777	3423	1127
	Elasticity	Value of Time US$/hr							
Optimum Toll (*in equivalent minutes*)	0.2	.90	5.475	8.023	8.596	7.558	6.015	4.008	1.259
	0.2	1.80	5.573	7.941	8.335	7.278	5.780	3.873	1.242
	0.8	.90	7.894	6.862	5.655	4.620	3.751	2.747	1.098
	0.8	1.80	8.001	6.753	5.531	4.473	3.610	2.634	1.063
	2.0	.90	9.188	6.372	4.751	3.686	2.940	2.167	0.950
	2.0	1.80	9.124	6.347	4.683	3.604	2.855	2.089	0.913
Optimum Toll (*US¢ per km*)	0.2	.90	8.212	12.034	12.894	11.336	9.022	6.011	1.889
	0.2	1.80	16.719	23.823	25.561	21.835	17.342	11.617	3.725
	0.8	.90	11.841	10.203	8.481	6.931	5.627	4.121	1.647
	0.8	1.80	24.002	20.259	16.592	13.420	10.830	7.903	3.189
	2.0	.90	13.782	9.558	7.126	5.529	4.409	3.250	1.425
	2.0	1.80	27.74	19.042	14.048	10.813	8.564	6.270	2.740
Optimum Flow (*veh/hr*)	0.2	.90	840.2	897.5	905.9	889.8	856.1	778.6	446.8
	0.2	1.80	843.3	896.2	902.2	884.7	849.5	771.0	442.2
	0.8	.90	895.4	875.1	845.8	808.4	763.7	685.9	402.2
	0.8	1.80	897.2	874.0	842.0	801.8	754.9	674.4	391.7
	2.0	.90	913.5	865.3	813.9	759.7	703.8	618.4	355.6
	2.0	1.80	914.1	864.7	811.0	754.5	696.2	607.6	343.1
Optimum Speed (*km/hr*)	0.2	.90	15.40	13.86	13.614	14.08	14.99	16.95	25.69
	0.2	1.80	15.32	13.89	13.72	14.22	15.16	17.14	25.83
	0.8	.90	13.92	14.48	15.26	16.21	17.31	19.22	27.13
	0.8	1.80	13.867	14.51	15.35	16.37	17.53	19.51	27.48
	2.0	.90	13.39	14.75	16.07	17.41	18.78	20.92	28.76
	2.0	1.80	13.37	14.76	16.14	17.54	18.97	21.19	29.23

Net Gain (time equivalent: minutes per km/hr)

0.2	.90	9,129	5,050	2,579	1,280	636	233	16
0.2	1.80	9,140	5,052	2,606	1,309	664	257	19
0.8	.90	9,394	5,098	2,866	1,663	979	453	51
0.8	1.80	9,401	5,105	2,871	1,686	1,002	482	57
2.0	.90	9,522	5,122	2,986	1,814	1,140	587	78
2.0	1.80	9,519	5,126	2,991	1,831	1,157	606	85

Net Gain (US$ per km/hr)

0.2	.90	136.93	75.75	38.68	19.20	9.49	3.50	0.25
0.2	1.80	274.21	151.55	78.19	39.27	19.93	7.72	0.58
0.8	.90	140.92	76.46	42.99	24.95	14.68	6.80	0.76
0.8	1.80	282.03	153.15	86.13	50.57	30.05	14.47	1.71
2.0	.90	142.82	76.83	44.79	27.22	17.10	8.82	1.18
2.0	1.80	285.58	153.77	89.73	54.94	34.71	18.18	2.56

Revenues (time equivalent: minutes per km/hr)

0.2	.90	4,600	7,201	7,787	6,725	5,149	3,120	563
0.2	1.80	4,700	7,117	7,521	6,439	4,911	2,986	549
0.8	.90	7,069	5,952	4,783	3,735	2,865	1,885	441
0.8	1.80	7,178	5,902	4,657	3,587	2,725	1,777	416
2.0	.90	8,394	5,514	3,866	2,800	2,069	1,340	338
2.0	1.80	8,453	5,488	3,798	2,720	1,987	1,270	313

Revenues ($ per km/hr)

0.2	.90	69.00	108.01	116.80	100.87	77.24	46.80	8.44
0.2	1.80	140.99	213.51	225.62	193.17	147.32	89.57	16.47
0.8	.90	106.03	89.28	91.73	56.02	42.97	28.27	6.62
0.8	1.80	215.34	177.07	139.70	107.61	81.75	53.30	12.49
2.0	.90	125.90	82.70	58.00	42.00	31.03	20.10	5.06
2.0	1.80	253.57	164.65	113.94	81.59	59.62	38.09	9.40

133

there is a very small diurnal variation and traffic consultants feel that network "capacity is deficient on many city streets."[36]

Relative importance of rural and urban traffic

The next important question is to examine the extent to which motor vehicles are used inside the urban area. It is clear that a substantial fraction of the vehicle kilometers do occur in the urban areas, but measurement involves many difficulties. A calculation for San Jose showed that from traffic counts approximately 25 percent of the total vehicle kilometers in the entire country occurred in a very small congested heart (1½ square kilometers) of the city. This small congested area comprised only 29 kilometers of city streets —which amount to only 5 percent of the total length of road in the metropolitan area, and probably less than one percent of the total all-weather roads in the country as a whole.

From San Salvador some useful statistics on the number of vehicles entering and leaving the central business district are available.[37] There were roughly 85,000 vehicle trips into the CBD daily, and about the same number out again. The total stock of vehicles in El Salvador was about 35,000—which implies that, on the average, each vehicle in the entire country took more than two trips a day into the CBD and out again. (These figures, of course, exclude those trips run solely in the CBD.) If the average distance in the urban congested area per trip were 5 kilometers, the 85,000 round trips per day would give rise to about 320 million vehicle kilometers. Since this figure does not take into account the concentrated operation of the considerable fleet of taxis inside the CBD, it is probably an underestimate. The total vehicle kilometers in El Salvador has been estimated from vehicle stock figures and traffic counts at 750 million. Thus it is likely that roughly 50 percent of the vehicle mileage occurs in the urban areas. This figure is broadly consistent with those derived from the congested heart of San Jose.[38] Indeed these two sets of statistics can be put together to suggest that at present levels of user charges, 25 percent of veh/km occur in the very heavily congested center, 15 percent in the lightly or moderately congested areas, and 60 percent on the uncongested interurban and rural highways.[39] If the structure of user charges were changed these proportions would also change according to the elasticities of demand.

---

[36] Adley Associates Inc. *Technical Report Transportation Study*. Ministerio de Obras Publicas: Direccion de Urbanismo y Arquitectura, El Salvador, 1968, pp. 41–42.

[37] Adley Associates, p. 40.

[38] This "heart" is a small fraction of the total urban area.

[39] In terms of resource allocation the urban areas are quantitatively more important than the rural areas because the cost of a vehicle kilometer is so much higher, except on rural earth roads.

The previous sections have estimated the costs of congestion attributable to users of urban road services. What remains to be calculated are the costs to the economy as a whole of the failure to impose these congestion charges or, looking at it another way, to calculate the benefits available through an imposition of these charges. Figure 7 illustrates the nature of the problem for situations where speeds exceed the maximum flow speeds. In the diagram DD' is the demand for urban street services, MC the marginal cost (excluding existing taxes) and PC the private cost (including existing taxes). The optimum congestion levy is SQ or SN above the existing tax and the output q_1. Abolishing the congestion levy increases output (veh/km) to q_2 and results in social costs exceeding private costs by TP. The resulting loss in surplus is given by the area STP.

The congestion cost estimated in the section above (9 cents per veh/km) is represented on the diagram by the distance $T'P$, that is, the 9 cents is a total congestion tax which includes the existing tax. In order to calculate the benefits foregone by not imposing congestion charges it would be necessary to know the shape of the demand curve DD'. Unfortunately this is an unknown and thus the gains from imposing a system of congestion charges can only be a matter of speculation.

If, for example, the demand for urban street services is perfectly inelastic

FIGURE 7
BENEFIT ATTRIBUTED TO IMPOSITION OF
A CONGESTION CHARGE

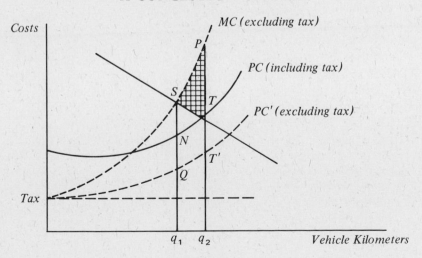

135

there will be no increase in surplus resulting from the imposition of congestion charges. Congestion does not change—all that happens is that government revenues increase. This in itself, however, may be considered as positive benefit if the congestion levy is regarded as one of a number of alternative sources of government revenue. If instead of raising revenues through congestion charges the government finances some of its expenditures through road user taxes in rural areas, the loss might be considerable. (See Chapter VI.)

Some idea of the costs of congestion can also be obtained by considering the costs of vehicle flows at various speeds. In the discussion of the costs of on-street parking an estimate of $1.4 million annually is presented as the benefits that could be achieved in San Jose by increasing urban speeds from the present congested peak speeds of 6 kph to 15 kph. This estimate excludes time costs. A conservative estimate of these time costs (see page 127) would double the size of the benefits. A similar degree of congestion exists in all five of the capital cities of Central America, so it would not be unreasonable to accept an estimate of 15 million dollars annually. This estimate is based on a reduction of the peak only. Congestion exists in all the cities over most of the day, and if the result of these charges is to reduce some of this congestion as well, the benefits will be correspondingly greater. Additional benefits could also be assigned to decreases in the accident rate, noise level, air pollution etc.

The reduction of congestion (or rise in speed) depends on the elasticity of demand. With the level of charges being proposed some elasticity is likely to exist, and given any degree of elasticity the benefits (in addition to the government revenues collected) quickly become substantial. It is difficult to quantify these benefits but the evidence suggests they might be quite large.

Pricing of Urban Street Services

Current policy

The existing road pricing arrangements for urban areas are primarily a consequence of the mixture of fuel taxes, license duties, and other user charges. These charges are not the result of any conscious policy formulation but simply the result of historical accident. It is difficult to state precisely the incidence of these charges on vehicle kilometers of urban travel because of the necessity of making quite arbitrary assumptions about the number of kilometers traveled, etc. Table 7.5, using some rough approximations, gives an idea of the incidence of "normal" user charges in urban areas. Passenger cars alone are considered as they are the major user of urban streets.

Aside from Costa Rica where much higher import duties are levied, user taxes are of the same order of magnitude for all of the countries. Fees for on-street parking change the distribution, but if off-street private parking

TABLE 7.5:   Present User Taxes for the Average Passenger Car in Urban Areas

(US cents per veh/km)

	User Taxes	On Street Parking Fees	Total
Guatemala	2.0	2.0	4.0
El Salvador	1.8	1.2	3.0
Honduras	1.7		1.7
Nicaragua	1.6		1.6
Costa Rica	4.1		4.1

Note: Based on assumptions of Table 5.9. Gasoline consumption increased by 25% to account for lower speed in urban areas. For parking charges, time of eight hours and average commute of 10 km 4 times daily.

TABLE 7.6:   Present User Taxes and Social Congestion Costs for the Average Passenger Car

(US cents)

	User Taxes	Costs	Difference
Guatemala	2.0	9.0	−7.0
El Salvador	1.8	9.0	−7.2
Honduras	1.7	9.0	−7.3
Nicaragua	1.6	9.0	−7.4
Costa Rica	4.1	9.0	−4.9

Source: Table 7.5 and text.

charges are included they are once again roughly similar. The typical bus probably pays user taxes somewhat similar to those of a seven-ton diesel truck, about 2.5 cents per veh/km in most of the countries. The incidence per passenger (or passenger seat) is, of course, much lower than for the seat of a passenger car.

The social costs of congestion estimated above were of the order of nine cents per kilometer at a speed of 15 kilometers per hour. The speed is higher that that of the most congested periods but probably represents an attainable average speed given some improvements in traffic engineering and law enforcement. To the extent that these improvements are not made, the cost estimate of nine cents per veh/km is, of course, an understatement.[40] This cost may then be compared with actual charges. (See Table 7.6)

Parking fees have not been included in the costs in Table 7.6 because of the arbitrary nature of their incidence. Only in two cities are on-street parking charges levied and even in these cities only over a limited area. The incidence thus depends on whether one is fortunate enough to find a free spot. If such

---

[40] Below 15 kph social congestion costs rise very rapidly. At 12 kph, for example, they reach 23 cents.

parking charges were more universal they would in most cases still not cover the social costs of the parked car, and could not be said to count as a payment for congestion caused by moving cars unless rates were drastically increased.

Regardless of whether or not parking charges are included, the conclusion is inescapable—users of urban streets are paying much less than the marginal costs of using the streets. The results of current policy, or better still current practices, are obvious. Central American cities are rapidly reaching a physical saturation point as to the volume of traffic that can be handled. Growth rates for urban traffic vary between eight and thirteen percent and at these growth rates even improvements in traffic engineering and law enforcement will only delay for a few years a completely chaotic situation. In Tegucigalpa the limit may have already been reached.

Congestion charges

The need to ration the use of existing urban road space in a more efficient manner is obvious. How this can be done is, however, a matter of some complexity. The ideal solution from a theoretical point of view is one in which each user of urban streets is asked to assume the costs to himself and to others which are generated by his use of the street. As was elaborated above, these costs vary considerably and would be different at various speeds and/or different times of the day. The user charge should thus be linked to each journey, that is, to the marginal decision to use or not to use the street. Other than by a system of metering vehicle kilometers or vehicle time in areas of varying degrees of congestion (in much the same manner as water or electric power is sold) it is difficult to conceive how this can be done. Regardless of the difficulties associated with techniques of pricing for these services, the problem of rationing scarce resources remains. Only rather blunt devices that can feasibly be administered are available within the existing institutional framework—but these are better than nothing at all. At later stages and when more experience has been gained with the relatively simple methods outlined below, more sophisticated pricing techniques may be worth attempting.

The simplest system for introducing some form of rationing of the use of urban streets is through the use of license duties and parking fees. In its most primitive form this could be a simple differential license duty between vehicles using streets in urban areas and those using rural highways. This is a crude measure, but if employed in conjunction with enforcement mechanisms and other tax measures it could be effective. The more restrictive the license fee is with respect to time and place, the closer it comes to approximating the required congestion charge. An annual license fee only intrudes on the decision to use urban streets on an annual basis. Once the fee has been paid there is no incentive to economize on use of streets. It does, however, eliminate some potential users from the congested area; because of the price some potential users will not license their vehicles for use in urban areas. The more frequently such a decision is required on the part of the road user the more accurately will scarce space be rationed. The license could thus be issued on a quarterly, monthly, weekly or perhaps daily basis. The frequency of issue could be a simple function of the costs of administration.[41] These costs do not appear to be prohibitive even for the issuance of daily licenses.

To make such a system of licensing work requires a greater degree of enforcement of traffic regulations than is currently the norm in Central America. This can be changed, however, and the large revenues generated from this type of license fee (part of which would defray the cost of collection) would provide a substantial incentive. The system of enforcement is relatively simple; all users of urban streets or those entering the metropolitan area during certain hours of the day are required to display either an appropriate license plate or windshield sticker.[42] Vehicles not displaying the appropriate license would then be subject to a fine of sufficient magnitude to discourage this form of tax avoidance.[43] Licenses issued on the basis of place of residence or business would be inappropriate as the differential in duties (see below) is of sufficient magnitude to encourage addresses of convenience.

These "urban street use" licenses could be sold in the form of a special plate to those requiring them on an annual (or perhaps a monthly) basis. Those who wish to purchase the license for shorter periods of time could do so by procuring the appropriate windshield sticker which could then be issued on a weekly or daily basis. In order to minimize the collection costs for the short period licenses, use should be made of existing retail outlets such as gasoline stations[44] that would be of convenience to motorists. Another technique that has been used recently in the City of Westminster (U.K.) to con-

---

[41] Included in these costs would be the costs born by the licensee in the form of time and inconvenience.

[42] It would be wasteful to require the license fee to be paid for use of the core area at night or in other times of low marginal congestion costs.

[43] The appropriate level of the fine is partly a matter of calculating the probabilities of getting caught. If the probability is one in ten trips then a fine equal to double the license fee would not be sufficient to discourage tax avoidance. The fine would have to be at least 10 times the license fee. This merely points out the obvious relationship between the fine and enforcement costs; the higher the fine, the lower the enforcement level required to deter excessive evasion. Too high a ratio of fine to license is, however, likely to lead to ill-feeling and charges of discriminatory enforcement.

[44] Other possibilities would include neighborhood stores, toll booths, traffic counting stations or police control point such as exist in Honduras and Guatemala.

trol resident parking could also be adapted for use as an urban congestion charge. In Westminster residents are issued with a monthly card in the form of a calendar. To park in the designated areas requires simply the placing of a previously purchased stamp (sold in books of various size) over the appropriate date on the calendar displayed in the window of the vehicle.[45] Users of urban streets could be required to display a similar calendar with a stamp placed over the appropriate date. A person desiring to take a trip into the congested area simply places a stamp over the date and displays the card in the window of the vehicle. This system has greater flexibility and could be administratively less costly than the system of issuing daily, weekly, monthly, etc. licenses.[46]

The exact method of selling these licenses or stamps would depend on the existing institutions in each country. They could, for example, be sold wholesale to gasoline stations with the market (through competition between stations) being allowed to establish the retail price.[47] Most of the administrative costs are thus covered by the gasoline stations themselves with the right incentives to keep costs to a minimum. Another technique would be for the authorities to set the retail price and provide a suitable margin for the retailers —much as is done in the case of postage or fiscal stamps.

More elaborate forms of restrictive licenses can also be applied, but these are not likely to be worth the additional costs. Different licenses (or stamps, or tabs) could be required, for example, for entering different zones of the city with different levels of congestion. This, of course, very quickly multiplies the collection and enforcement costs.

The administrative techniques are available; it is now a matter of establishing the rates. The marginal congestion costs[48] per vehicle kilometer for various speeds on the following page are based on the data for San Jose, Costa Rica. At a speed of less than 10 kph (the speed of the maximum flow) an additional vehicle actually reduces the volume of traffic and thus increases costs astronomically. Between speeds of 9 and 12 kph costs are high because the elasticity of speed with respect to flow is high (−9 at 10 kph, or a one percent decrease in volume increases speed by 9 percent) and the elasticity of costs with

---

[45] Once placed on the calendar these stamps are impossible to remove without being damaged.

[46] Still another possibility is to indicate the usage by tearing out a tab—the value of the unused portions could then be credited against purchase of further licenses.

[47] This is a familiar mechanism in Central America, and is most commonly applied to the sale of lottery tickets.

[48] Excluding non-working time.

Speed (kph)	Cost per Vehicle Kilometer (in US cents)
10	83
11	38
12	23
13	16
14	12
15	9
20	4
25	2

respect to flow is also high (7 at 10 kph, or a one percent decrease in flow de-decreases costs by 7 percent). These costs are probably understated due to the exclusion of the value of non-working time. Even so the congestion costs at speeds of less than 15 kph are quite impressive.

The problem is one of selecting the appropriate vehicle kilometer rate to be approximated by means of license duties. Here the best that can be done on the basis of existing information is to select what might be termed a representative level of congestion. During the congested peak periods where speeds of 4 to 10 kph are encountered, the costs are so high that the elasticity of the demand curve cannot be ignored; thus an attempt to approximate the congestion charge on the basis of present conditions would lead to a charge well above the optimum. The license duty is too blunt an instrument in this case. It is probably safer to select a speed representative of "normal" congestion and leave the solving of the peak problem to other instruments. In San Jose the average non-peak speed in the urban area is 15 kph. Other cities in Central America appear to have roughly similar average speeds (see page 121). This implies a congestion charge of 9 cents per vehicle kilometer. At 9 cents per veh/km the costs of heavy downtown congestion would be understated and the costs of the more suburban running overstated. Taking into account that this figure excludes a value for non-working time, it appears on balance to be as reasonable an estimate as it is possible to make.[49]

To change this 9 cents per veh/km into a license fee requires some averaging of trips per day and distance traveled. No accurate information is available for this purpose; the best that can be done is to make some rough guesses based on existing fragmentary information. On the basis of the location of suburbs (where most car owners are located) in Central American cities an average

---

[49] This is, of course, a matter of judgment. Better data would make a more refined judgment possible.

trip of 10 kilometers does not appear unreasonable.[50] The long traditional lunch period means that the average commuter makes two round trips daily[51] for a total of 40 kilometers per day. This amounts to a charge of US$3.60 per day at 9 cents a vehicle kilometer or $19.80 per week (5½ days). On the assumption of 264 working days this would mean an annual fee of approximately US$950 in Costa Rica; this would mean slightly more than doubling current user charges (for the average passenger car) from 4 cents a vehicle kilometer to 9 cents a vehicle kilometer. In other Central American cities it would mean a more than five-fold increase in user charges.

The net financial impact on the user of a vehicle is less than that stated above if non-urban running is also priced at marginal costs. The present total of annual charges in Cost Rica—on the assumption of 15,000 kilometers per annum per vehicle at 4 cents per kilometer (see Table 5.9) amounts to $600 per year. If 10,000 of these kilometers are done in urban areas at a price of 9 cents per kilometer and 5,000 in rural areas at 0.1 cent a kilometer, the total annual charge would be $905, or about half that being currently paid. Non-urban users of roads would, of course, be paying a much lower annual sum.

The next question is the license fee for buses and taxis. Buses cause more congestion than a private car but much less congestion per passenger carried. In calculations of congestion cost,[52] one bus is approximately equivalent to between 2 and 4 private cars. This suggests that a license fee be levied that is 2 to 4 times the passenger car fee. There are, however, good reasons for keeping the license fee on buses down to more modest levels. The most persuasive are the fact that buses are good substitutes for private cars and they cause much less congestion per passenger carried. Also, the majority of bus passengers are working and lower middle classes and there is a "distribution of income" argument for keeping the license duty down.

For taxis these reasons are not so persuasive. Although they are not so completely the preserve of the affluent as is true in some other societies, the majority of the poor either walk or ride the bus—they rarely use a taxi. Taxis do not take up much valuable parking space but they do interfere severely with traffic flow as they pick-up and set-down. Although these problems are best tackled by administrative regulations, there is clearly no good reason to reduce the taxi license fee below that of the car.

The above has only been worked out in terms of a license fee. It should

---

[50] Distances are probably shorter in the case of Tegucigalpa but then vehicle speeds are much lower.

[51] See also the data for El Salvador.

[52] For various estimates of the passenger car equivalents of buses, trucks, cyclists, etc., see *Road Research 1964*, HMSO, 1966.

also be possible to collect some of this 9 cents per kilometer by means of other taxes—particularly as some taxes will be required from non-urban users and as other taxes may be more closely linked with use. The most obvious choice here is the fuel tax. To approximate the economic user charge of 0.1 cent per kilometer in non-urban areas, a fuel tax of 4.7 cents per gallon would be required.[53] This 4.7 cents per gallon would then be a small fraction of the urban congestion charge. On top of this could be added an additional five cents per gallon regional tax,[54] making the total fuel tax in urban areas 9.7 cents per gallon or 0.25 cents a vehicle kilometer. Tire taxes, import duties, sales taxes and other traditional road user taxes cannot be used effectively here because they do not specify the area of use. This still leaves a large percentage to be covered by means of the license duty.

Parking fees. Some of the peak in the daily flow can be eliminated by means of parking charges. There are two reasons for doing this; one, a large part of the peak is attributable to commuter traffic which requires parking space; and two, to the extent that this parking takes place on the streets it blocks use of this space not only for others desiring to park but also for others desiring to use the streets for movement of vehicles. Information available is insufficient for estimating what the level per parking space on any particular street should be. If however the assumption is made that on-street parking causes a slow-down in vehicle speeds, some idea of the costs of this policy can be estimated and an argument can be made for recouping at least some of these costs through parking fees. Assuming that 30 percent[55] of the 53 million annual vehicle kilometers in the central business district in San Jose experience speeds of 6 kph in heavy congestion, the gains (or alternatively the costs) of raising this speed to 15 kph by reducing parking can be estimated as follows:

$$\text{Cost per veh/km at } 6 \text{ kph} = 2.8 + \frac{93}{6} = 18.3 \text{ cents}$$

$$\text{Cost per veh/km at } 15 \text{ kph} = 2.8 + \frac{93}{15} = 9.0 \text{ cents}$$

The saving in costs is thus 9.3 cents a vehicle kilometer. Over a total of 16 million vehicle kilometers per year this would amount to an annual saving (or cost) of 1.4 million dollars.

---

[53] Average passenger car at 40 kph consumes 0.0805 litres per kilometer (de Weille) on a paved tangent road. A tax of 0.1 cent/kilometer thus amounts to 4.7 cents per gallon.

[54] The five cent figure was used here because actual price differences between contiguous regions of this magnitude currently exist without noticeable fuel carrying. This type of regional tax also appears administratively feasible.

[55] This is merely a judgment, and probably on the conservative side. The evidence points to heavy congestion in the CBD over most of the day.

The 1.4 million dollars is at best a very crude estimate but it does indicate the magnitude of the costs of on-street parking if this parking means a loss of vehicle running space. Assuming that there are four hours per day five and a-half days a week of this congestion level,[56] this implies a minimum rental charge of 29 cents per hour during the peak periods for each of the 4,000 on-street parking spaces in the central business district of San Jose.[57] The charge during off-peak periods would be lower, but at each time the minimum value of the parking space would be its alternative use, that is, its use for running rather than parking vehicles. It should be stressed that these are minimum values for parking fees; they merely reflect the minimum supply price of parking space. It is quite possible that a higher price may be necessary to effectively ration existing space.

Parking fees may not provide the least cost solution, however. There are discontinuities in the supply and demand functions for both parking space and road use that may make the costs of collection prohibitively expensive. Parking space sold to a vehicle in the middle of a block during the peak period will be very expensive if that vehicle is the only one parked on the block. The vehicle effectively blocks a whole lane of traffic which may extend for some distance, thereby causing a lot of very expensive congestion. In these cases it may be administratively simpler just to prohibit parking completely by fiat rather than through the price mechanism of the market place. This is likely to be the situation in most Central American cities during peak periods. The only way to increase traffic speeds may be to prohibit parking completely on certain streets. This will improve the traffic flow but not public revenues.

Aside from their use in controlling peak congestion, parking fees could also be used to approximate part of the "normal" congestion charge. This assumes that the demand for road use and parking space is a joint demand—not an unreasonable assumption if commuter traffic is a substantial part of the traffic flow. In this case parking fees could be substituted for a system of restrictive licenses. A parking fee of $3.60 per day would thus be an effective substitute for a daily license fee of the same amount. This again could be administered in much the same fashion as the license fee. Cars parked on city streets would be required to display the appropriate license plate or windshield sticker.[58] There are, however, several disadvantages to the parking fee: not all of the

---

[56] Again a judgment but not an unreasonable one given the two round trips made daily by commuters.

[57] 1,210 congested hours per year at a rate of $1,157 per hour spread over an estimated 4,000 on-street parking spaces in the CBD.

[58] This system appears to be preferable to the use of parking meters where collection and administrative costs are high. It is also much more flexible.

revenue will accrue to the government,[59] and it is conceivable that at the level of parking charges envisaged chauffeurs[60] will be used to drive occupants into town and drive the vacant car out again to where free parking is available, thereby increasing congestion. Parking fees are therefore likely to be of limited use in levying congestion charges.

Administrative alternatives to parking meters. Parking meters are expensive in terms of capital (and foreign exchange) requirements. It is sensible therefore to examine feasible alternative arrangements that are less expensive and perhaps more suitable for Central America. The rationing of scarce parking space may be achieved by means of a parking-card or parking-disc system. Each month a card would be purchased with a perforated "stamp" for each day of the month. The motorist would have to tear off the appropriate day stamp if he wishes to occupy one of the designated parking places. At the end of the month the motorist would be credited for the days for which the stamps were still intact. This sum would be deducted from the purchase price of next month's card. It is possible to combine this card system with a "disc" system, where the time at which parking begins is indicated on a clock-face in the windscreen. The stamps may then be issued for one hour, two hours, or all day—and the police could inspect the disc to see whether there was any infringement.[61]

In the case of Central America the majority of parkers are commuters, and thus it seems sensible first of all to make the system as simple as possible. The parking stamp would give authority for the day's parking in a specified set of locations. For those parking places designed for short-period parking, parking meters could be retained but with sharply increased rates. Any expansion of restricted short-term parking would better be provided for through a license or stamp system.[62]

---

[59] Some parking will be provided in off-street private lots and the higher the charge the more attractive it will be to divert land into parking lots. The government could conceivably tax parking lots to recoup some of the rent but the revenues from this tax would be less than that from the license duty because private lots would have to earn a rent equal to that obtainable in alternative uses (e.g., buildings). If, however, the demand were inelastic (not likely to be the case if supply is given sufficient time to react) it might be possible to recoup the same revenues through parking charges.

[60] At parking charges of $3.60 a day it would pay to use chauffeurs in countries where the wage rate is less than 50 cents an hour.

[61] The yellow disc system has operated for sometime in certain European cities —but normally not for payment. The card system is used in certain London boroughs—Westminster and shortly in Islington. The evidence suggests that these systems are feasible and relatively cheap to operate.

[62] Some unattended lots operate by requiring customers to purchase a time-stamped card from a slot machine and display this in their car. Such a system

It may be convenient administratively to combine this parking card system with the restricted license arrangements discussed above. One card may be used to perform both tasks. Some fine points of pricing may be lost by such an integrated system, but the advantage of administrative simplicity and cheapness may well counterbalance such a loss.

Non-commuter traffic. Up to this point the discussion of congestion charges has been in terms of commuter traffic. Vehicle kilometers and congestion licenses were estimated on the basis of typical commuter distances. While this type of traffic is of considerable magnitude, it is not the only type of traffic using urban streets. Taxis and other commercial vehicles use urban streets extensively and license fees based on commuter distances would not accurately reflect this use. This traffic is, however, as much a contributor to urban congestion as the commuter traffic. Here again the best that can be done is to use crude averages to approximate the appropriate charges. Taxis could, for example, pay a license fee based on average daily (or monthly, annual, etc.) kilometers traveled in urban areas. No information is available as to the average vehicle kilometers traveled by taxis or commercial delivery vans, but this information would be relatively easy and cheap to obtain and could be used as the basis for issuing commercial licenses in the urban areas.[63]

The use of urban streets by buses can probably be estimated with a greater degree of accuracy. Buses keep regular schedules and routes, and on the basis of these it should be possible to estimate the appropriate congestion license. There is, however, a problem that is unique to buses (and to some extent taxis)—the problem of stops. In the narrow streets typical of Central American cities a bus stopping to pick up or discharge passengers effectively blocks the street causing considerable congestion. The situation is magnified by having many bus routes converge in one area, with the result that several blocks at a time may be jammed up with parked buses. One possible solution to this problem is an administrative one—to prohibit such convergences of routes or to provide suitable off-street facilities. (Such as is the case in Guatemala City where interurban buses are not allowed to converge on the city centre but have a separate facility on the outskirts of the city.) Another possible solution is to attach a charge for the use of bus stops and allow bus operators to determine their optimum route and whether or not to provide their own off-street facilities. High "stopping" fees could be attached to the use of scarce space in

could be adapted to curb parking where it would be more flexible and less costly than individual parking meters.

[63] The impact of heavy cargo vehicles on urban congestion has been ignored in this discussion for lack of adequate data. In any case they constitute only a small fraction of total vehicle kilometers (2 percent in San Jose).

the central business district. These would then be reflected in higher fares and would discourage passengers from demanding delivery to the core of the central area. Distances are short in most of the cities and an increased walk of a few blocks is a feasible alternative.

Taxis present a similar problem. At present taxis pick up and discharge passengers from the middle of one-lane streets completely blocking traffic. Taxis could be required to stop only at specified reserved places, the rent of which could be incorporated into the taxi license. Similar measures could also be used to control movement of commercial cargo vehicles. Loading zone privileges could be bought with the rate varying with the time of day.[64] Such a system has already been proposed in San Salvador and requires only the enacting legislation.

Enforcement

The installation of an effective system of congestion charges would be made more effective with a higher level of law enforcement than is currently the case in most Central American cities. Difficulties can be traced to three factors: poor quality of the enforcement staff, legal and constitutional obstacles and poor administration. The first and third of these are intimately linked. The only way they can be overcome is by a general upgrading of the quality and the number of the personnel involved. This requires more resources, and part of the revenues of the congestion levies should be directed toward this end. Higher salaries for enforcement officers would help prevent the present commonplace usage of "unofficial transfers" as a means of avoiding legal penalties.

Administration of traffic and traffic regulations is poor in all Central American cities. It is not so much a problem of corruption as one of just plain inefficiency. In San Jose, for example, the common practice is for traffic policemen to remove license plates from vehicles involved in traffic offenses. In order to redeem the plates the penalty must be paid. The paying of penalties is made so complicated that intermediaries have developed to perform this service. A car driving up to the courts with no plates is immediately set upon by numerous persons offering to redeem the plates for a fee (which often is less than the legal penalty). This type of procedure is wasteful and unnecessary; a simple billing of the owner of the offending vehicle would suffice. If the bill is not paid no plates are issued the following year to that vehicle.[65] This is not done at present because traffic penalties are not cross-referenced to vehicle registrations, a matter only of comparing lists. Some attention to administrative procedures could thus improve enforcement of traffic regulations.

---

[64] Outright prohibitions during peak hours may be administratively more feasible.

[65] This procedure could also be followed with respect to drivers' licenses.

147

Improvements in personnel and administrative procedures will not solve all of the problems of enforcement. Steps must also be taken to overhaul the rather archaic legal structure. The present legal structure was not designed to accommodate a modern system of traffic enforcement. Procedures are excessively complicated and slow with the result that a premium is placed upon "unofficial" settlements. The levying of fines for traffic infractions should be an almost automatic procedure with a given penalty associated with a given offense. This—in contrast to the present system where the penalty is a debatable issue—would discourage the excessive use of an already overburdened judicial system.

The system of congestion charges proposed by this study should not require much additional effort in the area of law enforcement. The techniques are simple; what is required is the political will.

Conclusions

The data

The data available for analyzing the problem of urban congestion and congestion charges are not always as detailed nor as precise as would be desirable, but then neither are the instruments for levying these charges very sharp. The conclusions and suggestions of this chapter are couched in very general terms. Only broad orders of magnitude are indicated and these are based mainly on the data available for San Jose. This should not, however, be interpreted as an indication of the impracticality of the suggestions. Most of the necessary data would be easy and inexpensive to collect. It has never been collected only because no reason was ever conceived for doing so. The fact that some of the data has been collected recently in San Jose (and on a more fragmentary basis in other cities) is an indication of the growing awareness of the problems of the cities.

The remarkable similarity between traffic conditions in the various urban areas also enables the attachment of a high degree of confidence to the generalization of the experiences of one urban area. This is further strengthened by the similarity of much of this data to conditions found all over the world. Costs and the techniques involved in the production of motor vehicles and road services do not seem to vary significantly from country to country.

The congestion charges

The conclusion is inescapable that the costs of congestion are high. The exact amount to be charged is a more debatable point. The judgment based on the analysis above is that a charge of 9 cents per vehicle kilometer might be an appropriate amount to use as an initial basis. Further research may indicate that a charge of 7, 8, or perhaps 10 cents may be more appropriate in some cities. In any case, the gradual introduction of these charges will allow time to find the most suitable level of charges.

The method for collecting these charges can also be subject to some variation to take into account the political and institutional factors in each country. In some cases higher parking fees may be more appropriate than license duties or vice versa. The degree of complexity of these charges will also depend on the institutional framework in each country. The bias in the suggestions of this chapter have been towards simplicity; undue complexity in initiating a system of congestion charges may cost more than the doubtful benefits that would be gained.

The congestion charges suggested here should also be regarded only in the context of the total system of user charges. It is only in this context that the economic rationale behind the taxes suggested (as opposed to the level of the charge) is clear. The implications of economic user charges in both urban and rural areas are discussed further in Chapter VIII together with the rate of timing of their implementation and their impact on government revenues.

Administration

The local nature of the congestion charge and the substantial revenues that would be collected raise some questions as to how and by whom they should be administered. The current poor quality of local government raises some doubts as to their ability to administer a system of congestion charges or to spend the resulting revenues efficiently. The solution to the problems of local government appear to lie in a better tax base and a general improvement of the quality of administration. These are to a large extent dependent on each other. Low revenues have meant low salaries which in turn have meant that local governments have not been able to attract high quality personnel. The poor quality of local governments has often been given as the reason for denying them further revenues; the revenues, it is alleged, would only be wasted in the hands of local governments. This may well be true given the current structure of municipal government, but the argument is a circular one with no solution; to break the cycle additional revenues are a prerequisite.

There are no a priori reasons why certain services (such as roads) should be provided by local rather than the national government. Indeed a strong argument can be made, particularly in a small country, for providing many services on a national scale. This is the observable trend in Central America. Various decentralized or autonomous agencies have been established to provide water, power, sewerage, public wefare, etc. This, given the economies of scale inherent in public utilities of this type, probably more than compensates for

149

the loss of local initiative and control. At some point, however, local governments reach a size sufficient to enable them to take advantage of these economies of scale, and with their greater sensitivity to local issues they are then in a position to provide a better level of services.

Most local governments in Central America are not of sufficient size to be able to administer public services efficiently. The exceptions to these are the capital cities in each country which have grown large enough to make more comprehensive local government economically feasible. The inability of the central government in each country to deal adequately with the problems of the rapidly growing urban centers suggests that not only is better local government economically feasible, but it is probably necessary if the urban problems are to be solved. The central government tends to be preoccupied with many issues on a national scale and gives low priority to local problems.

The present system in which the responsibility for provision of local services is either divided or mixed is probably the worst combination conceivable. The poor condition of urban streets, for example, cannot be attributed to any level of government or more importantly to any politically responsive unit within the government. Local authorities claim they have no revenues (the central government takes them all), and the central government says that it has other pressing needs or more commonly that it is a responsibility of the local government. In most of the countries in Central America it would be extremely difficult for a group of neighbors to get a street improved even though they were willing to tax themselves in order to pay for it.

In the case of urban streets ample opportunity exists for collecting large additions to local revenues which at the same time would aid in solving some of the traffic problems. Congestion charges might thus provide the means of breaking out of the downward historical spiral of local government revenues and quality of service. Care would, of course, have to be taken to insure that the transfer of revenues to local governments does not create fiscal difficulties for the central government. In some countries revenue from the congestion levies could be used as a substitute for transfer payments already being received by local governments. These revenues might also substitute for any planned additional expenditures of the central government in urban areas.

150

VIII

CONCLUSIONS AND RECOMMENDATIONS

General Considerations

In order to maximize benefits, road services should be priced so as to equate price to the opportunity costs of providing the service. This means a price equal to the variable maintenance costs plus the social congestion costs caused by an additional vehicle using a kilometer of road. This is the prescription of theory and should be the goal of pricing policy when the sole concern is the efficiency of the economy. The preceding chapters have analyzed the system of road user charges within this frame of reference. From this analysis a reasonably clear picture emerges of the "ideal" system of road user charges.

The "ideal" system in the Central American context should be one in which substantial charges are exacted in urban areas and only small levies are imposed on uncongested rural facilities. It has not been possible to indicate the precise level of these charges. It has only been possible to suggest orders of magnitude. This is, however, sufficient to formulate a plan for improving the current system of road user charges. The estimates of these charges are of sufficient accuracy to indicate the direction of change. The necessary changes will take time and should be carried out slowly to provide the necessary information and experience to permit the formulation of more precise pricing policies.

151

Pricing of uncongested facilities

Approximately three-quarters of the vehicle kilometers in Central America experience what can be described as uncongested conditions. These vehicle kilometers should then be priced at a level sufficient to cover the variable maintenance costs. Estimates of variable maintenance costs were presented in Chapter IV, but such figures leave much to be desired. They are, however, sufficiently consistent with data from other countries so as to permit some confidence in their general validity. The most important omission in these estimates is the lack of information on the variable maintenance costs caused by vehicles of different weights. There is some evidence that suggests that heavier vehicles cause more damage, but it is not possible to say how much more damage is done by a twenty-ton truck than a five-ton truck. It should be possible, however, to obtain this information inexpensively and over a relatively short period of time.

On the basis of the average of costs over all vehicle types, the evidence is overwhelmingly in support of the contention that uncongested vehicle kilometers are overpriced, at least for paved roads. This overpricing ranges from about 60 percent for light vehicles (passenger cars and trucks under one-ton capacity) to about 20 percent for the 5 to 7-ton truck. The analysis of Chapter VI suggests that this might be important in terms of its costs in output foregone if unemployed resources exist that need land as the complementary factor to bring them into productive use. The cost may also be considerable in terms of the investments not made in specific projects because of an insufficient rate of return, the cause of which is the high taxes on road services in general rather than lack of an adequate economic rate of return.

Pricing of congested facilities

In Chapter VII the costs of urban congestion were found to be considerable and in all probability they will continue to grow over time. Unless cities are almost completely reconstructed—a prohibitively costly task—the only alternative appears to be a better rationing of existing facilities. This can be done through a better system of pricing for use of street facilities both for travel and parking, as well as through improved traffic engineering and law enforcement.

The data on costs suggest that the price for the use of urban streets should double in the case of Costa Rica and increase by four to five times in the other countries. These cost estimates are crude, but with a modest expenditure on collecting information they could be much improved. It is not proposed that charges be suddenly increased to the level of costs but rather that they be raised in steps over a period of time. This will provide better cost estimates and develop the experience required to administer a system of congestion charges.

An important effect of the congestion charges will be an increase in tax revenues. Strong arguments can be found (see page 149) for turning most of the revenues over to the city government (in lieu of current subsidies), not only for maintenance of streets but also for other much needed urban expenditures. In most cases this would require a greater degree of efficiency in urban administration. This will take time but the provision of increased revenues will add the necessary impetus for accomplishing this task.

User Charges: The Instruments Available

It is difficult to divorce the changes in levels of taxes or user charges from the instruments available to implement these charges. "General" levels of charges must be translated into recommendations about specific taxes. Each tax can then be discussed in terms of the impact on resource allocation. What types of taxes should be levied, how should they be levied, and what should be the exact level of each tax?

Fuel taxes

At present fuel taxes are by far the most important element in the system of user charges. A shift towards pricing of road services at their opportunity cost will tend to reduce the importance of fuel taxes as contributors to public revenue because of the difficulties of associating the incidence of these taxes with the different use of road services. It is suggested that fuel taxes be used as the primary means of approximating the economic user charge on uncongested roads. Because of the difficulties associated with pricing for different road surfaces, this means in effect using the fuel tax as an approximation to the price of using paved roads.

The variable maintenance costs caused by the "average" vehicle is roughly 0.1 cents per kilometer, which implies the following fuel tax per gallon for the vehicle categories listed below:

TABLE 8.1: Fuel Tax Required to Approximate EUC of 0.1 Cent per Vehicle Kilometer on Paved Roads

(US cents)

Average Passenger Car	4.7 per gallon
One-Ton Truck (Gas)	3.4
7-Ton Truck (Gas)	1.3
7-Ton Truck (Diesel)	2.0
18-Ton Truck (Diesel)	1.5

Note: Same assumptions as Table 5.9.

From this table it can be seen that the incidence of a specific tax of 0.1 cents per gallon varies considerably for the different types of vehicles. This cannot be avoided because it would be administratively too difficult and too expensive to distinguish between types of vehicles. The best that can be done is to make the distinction between those using diesel and those using gasoline. A tax at the level required to approximate the costs of an average passenger vehicle has a higher incidence on the trucks; but this is not undesirable if, as is probable but not proven, the trucks generate much heavier variable road maintenance costs. The following would be the incidence per vehicle kilometer of a five-cent per gallon gasoline tax and a two-cent per gallon diesel tax:

TABLE 8.2:   Incidence of a Five-Cent per Gallon Gasoline and Two-Cent per Gallon Diesel Tax

(paved roads, US cents)

	Tax Incidence (*Per veh/km*)	No. of Times Greater than that of Average Passenger Car
Average Passenger Car	0.11	–
One-Ton Truck (Gas)	0.15	1.5
7-Ton Truck (Gas)	0.40	3.6
7-Ton Truck (Diesel)	0.10	–
18-Ton Truck (Diesel)	0.14	1.3

The effect of this tax would be that a one-ton truck would be paying a tax 1.5 times as great as that of an average passenger car, a seven-ton truck 3.6 times as great. While the truck-car differential in variable maintenance costs is not known, the above price structure does not seem greatly inconsistent with the cost structure, at least for gasoline vehicles. For diesel powered vehicles the price is likely to understate the costs. Adjusting the diesel tax so that a seven-ton diesel truck pays the same amount as a seven-ton gasoline truck implies a tax of 8.0 cents per gallon of diesel with an incidence of 0.5 cents per vehicle kilometer for the 18-ton truck. Since very few diesel passenger vehicles or small trucks are used, the overcharging of them is not likely to be of much consequence.

The conclusions are that the level of fuel taxes required to approximate the *EUC* in uncongested conditions is about 5 cents per gallon for gasoline and 8 cents per gallon for diesel. The fuel taxes were stated in terms of cents per gallon. To avoid difficulties associated with changes in the general price level it would be better to state these taxes as a percentage of price or as a percentage markup over costs.[1] The tax would have to take into account the different efficiencies of fuels of varying octanes. The best way to handle this

---

[1] The costs here should include the costs of the small refining operations if it has not been possible to pass these costs back to the crude oil margins.

154

would be to assume that the refining cost differences reflect the relative efficiencies of the fuels. The price ex refinery plus tax would then be as follows (in cents per gallons):

	Regular		Super		Diesel	
	Price	%	Price	%	Price	%
Price ex refinery[a]	10.5	67.7	12.5	67.7	8.6	51.9
Tax	5	32.3	6.0	32.3	8.0	48.1
Wholesale price	15.5	100.0	18.5	100.0	16.6	100.0

[a] Appropriate world refining costs. Assumes the inefficiencies of the refining operations are passed back to suppliers.

The tax would thus be stated as 32.3 percent tax on the ex refinery price of gasoline (assuming that the tax is collected at this level) and a 48.1 percent tax on diesel. The tax would be collected from the seller and taken out of the gross price.

In Chapter VII the possibility of using the fuel tax as part of the congestion levy was discussed. This means that fuel sales would have to be distinguished by area of sale. There do not appear to be any administrative obstacles to implementing a differential tax; it is already done in two countries and officials of the distributing companies and tax officials could not foresee any insurmountable obstacles. The possible differential varies from country to country. A five-cent differential is probably reasonable in open areas such as Managua and San Salvador and a greater differential is probably feasible in the more isolated urban areas of Tegucigalpa and Guatemala City. The relatively small use of urban streets by diesel fueled vehicles—together with the fact that most of them would have little difficulty in purchasing nearly all their fuel in the low rate areas suggests that this type of tax differential would not be worthwhile for diesel fuel.

In view of the fact that the move towards charging the opportunity costs for road use would result in lowering of the general level of fuel taxes, the establishment of this differential should not be difficult. In Honduras, for example, it would still mean the lowering of the fuel tax in the Central District by 4 cents.[2]

Tire taxes

Tires in Central America bear a relatively heavy burden. Much of the tax is used to support a tire industry of insufficient size to produce tires at competi-

---

[2] This may make the introduction of congestion levies more palatable politically and lessen taxpayer resistance.

tive world prices. Given the existence of the high cost domestic industry, it is doubtful whether it would be desirable to impose an additional tax burden on tires. Higher taxes on tires would create problems of enforcement as well as of public safety. If, however, changes are made in current policy with respect to the protection of the domestic tire industry, it would then be possible to use the tire tax as a means of reflecting the variable maintenance costs on different road surfaces. Since truck tires can be distinguished from those of automobiles, tire taxes can be used to charge heavy vehicles a higher price for the use of roads. The existence of the protected domestic tire industry thus limits the possibilities of a useful instrument of taxation of road users. Even if this were not the case, however, it would be desirable to examine further the effects of tire taxes on traffic accidents before making any recommendations.

Vehicle purchase taxes

The variable maintenance costs on uncongested roads can be best approximated by use of the fuel and (perhaps) tire taxes discussed above. Vehicle purchase taxes, whether in the form of import duties or domestic excises, are inappropriate as a means of dealing with urban congestion because of the difficulties in identifying vehicles that use only congested streets. This type of tax has many fiscal disadvantages. It is therefore proposed that these types of taxes be eliminated and a system of license fees be used in their place.[3]

The elimination of import duties has several advantages. In particular, by moving to license fees there would be a greater stability in government revenues. Revenues from import duties (and thus all purchase duties) vary considerably from year to year depending on changes in income, balance of payments problems, etc. This is due to the fact that the revenue comes from the increment to the stock of vehicles. When annual license duties are levied revenues come from the existing stock of vehicles. Aside from these purely fiscal or revenue advantages, the avoidance of these taxes will prevent distortions from arising in the size and composition of the vehicle fleet.

The elimination of import and sales taxes on vehicles should not be difficult in Central America. Duties are significant only on passenger vehicles; they are low on trucks and other commercial vehicles. In addition, except for a small-scale assembly operation in Costa Rica there is no domestic industry to protect. The impact of the elimination of these taxes on government revenues is discussed below, but it should be emphasized that simply to eliminate these taxes without replacing them by other measures would not be defensible.

---

[3] In cases where a general sales tax exists, this portion could remain so as not to change the rate of substitution between competing consumption goods.

License fees

At present license fees form an insignificant part of the system of user charges. The only cases where they are of importance are on large trucks in El Salvador and Guatemala. As was suggested in Chapter V these are perversely related to costs of road use. In the system of congestion charges proposed in Chapter VII, the license duty, in the form of specialized licenses, would become an important part of the user charge system. Indeed the license duties would be responsible for most of the revenues raised from user charges.

The system of license duties proposed in Chapter VII was strictly for urban areas and could be initially established at levels representing a charge of nine cents per vehicle kilometer travelled under congestion-prone conditions. As an annual charge for vehicles used fairly regularly within the congested area this would represent a fee totaling about 900 dollars a year. The fuel tax proposed above of 10 to 15 cents per gallon would form a very minor addition to the 900 dollar license fee (10–20 dollars).

The figure is very rough, and it is not suggested that it would be desirable to introduce this level of license fee immediately but rather over a period of time and as other types of vehicle charges are reduced. This would allow time to estimate the required level of congestion charges more accurately for the specific conditions of each city.

Summary of proposed user charges

The system of user charges that emerges from the above discussion is remarkably simple and should not present any insurmountable problems with respect to administration and implementation. There are two basic elements in the system: the fuel tax and license duties. The fuel tax would be the primary means of approximating the variable maintenance costs in rural areas, and the license duties the primary means of approximating the congestion costs in urban areas. These taxes should be substituted for the existing system of purchase duties, fuel taxes, license fees, tolls, etc.

The goal of this proposed system of prices is to approximate the opportunity costs of road use. This need not be the sole aim of policy and it is conceivable that road taxes offer means for raising government revenues preferable to other types of taxes. This possibility is discussed below.

The Proposed System: Revenues and the Implementation Process

The proposed system of fuel taxes plus urban license duties represents a considerable change from the existing structure of road taxes. For this reason and because of the uncertainty of some of the estimates, the process of adjustment should be a gradual one. The rate at which changes are introduced and how they are introduced is, of course, a matter of political judgment. The following proposals for the timing of these changes is, therefore, more of an illustrative exercise than a definite plan of action. In each case changes would have to be related to the revenue needs of the government and thus to the fiscal situation in each year.

In general it is suggested that increases in some taxes be accompanied by decreases in other taxes. As the direction of total taxes is generally upward, the lowering of some taxes will lessen taxpayer hostility to the changes and in addition produce a smoother path of adjustment in government revenues. The pattern of change is one of lowering gasoline taxes, raising diesel taxes, abolishing all license and purchase taxes except license duties in urban areas which would increase gradually, and retaining a nominal registration fee.

An illustrative five-year program together with its impact on government revenues (in millions of dollars) is summarized below:

	Guatemala	*El Salvador*	*Nicaragua*	*Costa Rica*

First Year

Reduce registration fees to a nominal level and raise special licenses in urban areas to approximate 1.5 cents a vehicle kilometer. Raise diesel tax to 8 cents per gallon. In El Salvador lower gas tax by 5 cents per gallon. Import duties decreased by 20 percent.

Fuel Tax Collection	9.3	4.9	3.6	5.4
Diesel	(1.0)	(0.9)	(0.4)	(1.1)
Gasoline	(8.3)	(4.0)	(3.2)	(4.3)
Congestion Charge	3.9	3.0	2.1	3.4
Purchase Taxes	3.6	2.8	2.1	1.8
Total	16.8	10.7	7.8	10.6

Second Year

Raise urban congestion charges by 1.5 cents a vehicle kilometer and lower gas tax by 5 cents per gallon. Decrease import duties 20 percent.

Fuel Tax Collection	7.4	3.9	2.7	4.4
Diesel	(1.0)	(0.9)	(0.4)	(1.1)
Gasoline	(6.4)	(3.0)	(2.3)	(3.3)
Congestion Charge	7.7	5.9	4.2	6.8
Purchase Taxes	2.7	2.1	1.6	1.3
Total	17.8	11.9	8.5	12.5

158

Third Year

Raise urban congestion charges by 1 cent, lower gas taxes by 5 cents in rural areas only, and lower import duties by 20 percent.

Fuel Tax Collection	6.1	3.1	2.1	3.8
Diesel	(1.0)	(0.9)	(0.4)	(1.1)
Gasoline (rural)	(3.0)	(1.2)	(1.1)	(1.6)
(urban)	(2.1)	(1.0)	(0.6)	(1.1)
Congestion Charges	10.3	7.9	5.6	9.1
Purchase Taxes	1.8	1.4	1.0	0.9
Total	18.2	12.4	8.7	13.8

Fourth Year

Raise urban congestion charges by one cent, lower import duties by 20 percent.

Fuel Tax Collection	6.1	3.1	2.1	3.8
Congestion Charges	12.8	9.8	7.0	10.4
Purchase Taxes	0.9	0.7	0.5	0.5
Total	19.8	13.6	9.6	14.7

Fifth Year

Raise urban congestion charges by one cent, abolish all import duties.

Fuel Tax Collection	6.1	3.1	2.1	3.8
Congestion Charges	15.4	10.9	8.4	13.7
Purchase Taxes	—	—	—	—
Total	21.5	14.0	10.5	17.5

Honduras has been excluded from the above summary because the existing system of charges requires smaller changes in its structure than is the case of the other countries. A possible pattern of change for Honduras in the first year would be to reduce license fees to a nominal registration fee and lower import duties by 20 percent. License fees in urban areas would be raised to approximate 15 cents a vehicle kilometer, the diesel tax raised to eight cents per gallon, and the gasoline tax lowered by four cents. The revenues would be as follows (in millions of dollars):

Fuel Tax Collection	3.0
Diesel	(0.9)
Gasoline	(2.1)
Congestion Charges	1.6
Purchase Taxes	0.7
Total	5.3

In the second year urban congestion charges would be raised by another 1.5 cents a vehicle kilometer and gasoline taxes could be lowered by five cents in rural areas. Revenues should be as follows:

Fuel Tax Collection	2.5
Diesel	(0.9)
Gasoline (rural)	(0.9)
(urban)	(0.7)
Congestion Charges	3.3
Purchase Taxes	0.5
Total	6.3

In the following years only congestion charges need to be raised to whatever levels appear appropriate. If the charges are raised to six cents a vehicle kilometer at the end of five years (the level of the other countries) total revenues would be 9.1 million dollars.

Public revenues

Revenue collections projected above must be viewed with caution. In most cases they are probably on the conservative side. They are based on existing volumes of traffic (1966) and merely show what would happen to tax collections if a different set of taxes were applied to this volume of traffic. This is unrealistic in the sense that some growth in traffic is to be expected as the economies grow.[4] The estimates are based on the data in Tables 3.1 and 5.9 which contain estimates of vehicle kilometers and fuel consumption. One-third of all gasoline consumption was assumed to take place in urban areas and no allowances were made for the slightly higher taxes to be placed on higher octane fuels. A different time path for the implementation of the suggested system of road user charges will alter the pattern of revenue collections. Considerable

---

[4] If there is some elasticity in the demand for urban street use the conservative bias is necessary as most of the revenues are raised on these streets. It is likely to be more relevant in the later years when the congestion charges are higher, than in the early years when the charges are being introduced.

TABLE 8.3: Revenues from Proposed System of User Charges

(million US$)

	Present Level	1st Year	2nd Year	3rd Year	4th Year	5th Year	Compound Rate of Growth (from 1966)
Guatemala	17.4	16.8	17.8	18.2	19.8	21.5	4.3
Honduras	3.6	5.3	6.3	7.1	8.1	9.1	20.2
El Salvador	10.6	10.7	11.9	12.4	13.6	14.0	5.7
Nicaragua	6.0	7.8	8.5	8.7	9.6	10.5	11.9
Costa Rica	10.1	10.6	12.5	13.8	14.7	17.5	10.5

scope exists here for tailoring the transition to the fiscal needs of the government.

One of the implicit thoughts behind the suggested pattern of implementation was the fiscal needs of the governments. For most of the Central American countries the need for additional public revenues continues to be a pressing problem, and taxation of road users offers an attractive way of raising some of these revenues. The above program has built-in increases in revenue but at the same time has kept the tax structure within the bounds of the proposed system of economic user charges. (See Table 8.3.) If this rate of increase should prove to be greater than what is politically acceptable, the possibility always exists of either slowing up the rate of increase of the congestion charges or alternatively lowering fuel and purchase taxes at a faster rate.

On the other hand, should it be considered politically expedient to raise even more revenues from the road-using public, this could be done. The costs of doing so would, however, have to be carefully investigated.[5] It thus might be desirable to maintain the existing level of fuel taxes in rural areas. The disadvantage of this is, of course, that the trade-off between lowering some taxes and raising others is lost. This may increase the difficulties in making a system of congestion charges acceptable to the taxpayer.

A preferable way of taxing simply for the sake of raising government revenues (as opposed to charging road users for the cost of road services) would be by use of either sumptuary taxes on vehicle purchases or better still by applying a surcharge to the urban congestion license duty. The present system of import duties for passenger automobiles contains some elements of a sumptuary tax. The preferable system, however, would be to raise these revenues

---

[5] There is sufficient evidence to suggest that underemployed factors exist and thus the costs, in resource foregone, of this type of taxation might be considerable. See Chapter VI.

161

(US$)

| | Additional Revenue (*millions of dollars*) | Annual License Fee per Vehicle if Burden Distributed to: | |
		Passenger Vehicles Only	All Vehicles
Guatemala	5.8	196	94
Honduras	1.2	113	64
El Salvador	3.5	158	86
Nicaragua	2.0	210	72
Costa Rica	3.4	210	82

Source: Tables 3.2 and 3.9.

through the license fee. If, for example, it was considered desirable to raise an additional one-third more revenues from road users, license fees would have to be raised annually by the amounts listed in Table 8.4. Two options are presented here: one in which the burden is equally distributed to all vehicles, and the other where it is distributed to passenger vehicles only (assuming that passenger travel is a form of consumption). These fees would be in addition to the proposed congestion charges. Other distributions are also possible. The license fee could be higher on luxury vehicles or on vehicles used in urban areas (on the assumption of an inelastic demand). Care would have to be taken, however, to insure that distortions are kept to a minimum. Difficulties would be encountered if all the tax were shifted to passenger vehicles —substitution of light trucks for passenger vehicles tends to take place if the level of the license fee is sufficiently high.

The existence of a common market further complicates the using of road taxes as a means of raising public revenues. If trucks licensed in Honduras were subject to a higher license fee than those in the other countries, it would tend to shift the international carrying trade away from Honduran vehicles. Some form of tax harmonization would be required (see page 167).

Tax incidence

The previous section considered the impact of the suggested implementation plan on government revenues. This is an important consideration but is not the only one; the ultimate acceptability of the proposed scheme rests with the taxpayer. Table 8.5 shows the impact of the plan of implementation on the taxes paid by the owners of various categories of vehicles. It will be noted that the congestion charge by the fifth year only amounts to US$600 as compared with US$900 which was estimated as the desirable level in the previous chapter. Thus the full implementation of the proposed charges is not visualized by

162

TABLE 8.5: Annual Taxes[a] Paid by Class of Vehicle,[b] Five-Year Illustrative Implementation Plan

(US$)

	Average Passenger Vehicle			Seven-Ton Truck	
	Urban[e]		Rural[d]		
	Conges-tion	Other	Total	Gasoline Powered	Diesel Powered
Guatemala					
Current			276	276	1,513	773
1st Year	150	211	361	211	1,300	612
2nd	300	162	462	162	1,025	564
3rd	400	117	517	107	750	516
4th	500	83	583	73	716	468
5th	600	50	650	38	681	420
Honduras					
Current			232	232	1,025	220
1st Year	150	147	297	147	1,025	395
2nd	300	111	411	111	786	395
3rd	400	82	482	71	544	395
4th	500	62	562	51	544	395
5th	600	42	642	31	544	395
El Salvador					
Current			246	246	1,634	797
1st Year	150	186	336	186	1,239	636
2nd	300	142	442	142	960	582
3rd	400	102	502	92	681	528
4th	500	73	573	63	642	474
5th	600	44	644	34	604	420
Nicaragua					
Current			225	225	1,301	757
1st Year	150	165	315	165	1,189	804
2nd	300	123	423	123	879	708
3rd	400	86	486	75	569	612
4th	500	59	559	48	500	516
5th	600	33	633	22	430	420
Costa Rica					
Current			595	595	1,711	823
1st Year	150	472	622	472	1,560	951
2nd	300	358	658	358	1,230	823
3rd	400	247	647	223	894	696
4th	500	148	648	137	799	568
5th	600	50	650	38	703	441

[a] Includes tire taxes.
[b] Same assumptions as Table 5.9.
[e] Assumes 10,000 kilometers in urban area and 5,000 in rural or uncongested conditions.
[d] 15,000 kilometers in rural areas only.

the end of the fifth year; this would allow an evaluation of the impact of the measures to be undertaken.

Urban passenger vehicles. For the owners of passenger vehicles in urban areas, the shift to a system of congestion charges (with the exception of Costa Rica) represents a substantial increase in taxes paid.[6] This is unavoidable if the costs of congestion are to be reflected in the price paid. Not all of the increase is, however, a current cash outlay; part of the taxes paid represent an amortization of the import duty over the life of the vehicle. In Costa Rica where the highest import duties are levied, the import duties currently account for 472 of the 595 dollars annually paid in taxes. In Guatemala the corresponding amount is 170 out of 276 dollars. The switch from an import duty to a congestion charge has two effects on present owners of vehicles used in urban areas; first it subjects them to a capital loss, and secondly it increases their annual cash outlay. The first of these is actually realized only if the vehicle is sold. The stream of real services over the lifetime of the vehicle does not change, but because of the lower price of new cars the owner will be induced to scrap his vehicle earlier. If the vehicle is kept until it has zero value and a new vehicle is purchased at the lower price (no import duties), the psychological impact of the capital loss is minimized. Sale of the vehicle will subject the owner to an obvious capital loss. The actual loss increases at a rate somewhat greater than the 20 percent per year reduction in import duties, depending on the time preference of buyers and sellers.[7] The vehicle is, however, depreciating over time and as it approaches scrap value the capital loss decreases relative to the total price. One desirable impact of this change is that it will probably discourage the substitution of old cars for new imports; that is, rather than realizing the capital loss owners of vehicles will continue to hold on to them.[8] An offsetting factor of this capital loss is the ability of the owner to purchase a new vehicle at a lower price. It should also result in an improvement in accident statistics as the old vehicles are scrapped and new ones substituted.

The effect of this rather confused movement of capital values and actual cash outlays can be more clearly seen in the changes in government revenues in the case of Costa Rica. Government revenues increase at a rate of 10.5 percent per year (Table 8.3) even though the taxes paid by urban vehicle owners

---

[6] Taxis and other extensive users of urban streets should be subject to a higher license fee based on an estimate of average use (see p. 142).

[7] That is, there will be some buyers willing to wait one more year before purchasing the vehicle at a lower price.

[8] The loss has, of course, occurred whether the vehicle is sold or not. This is merely another form of the "money illusion."

increase by only 1.8 percent per year and taxes on all other vehicles decline. This is because the imposition of the congestion charge represents an increase in annual cash outlays, while the amortization of the import duty is merely the financial assignment on an annual basis of revenues already received by the government. These revenues represent the capital loss of the vehicle owner.

Rural passenger vehicles. The present owner of a vehicle used exclusively in non-congested conditions is subject to the same capital loss as the owner of a vehicle used in urban areas, but at the same time he is compensated in part for this loss by a continual decline in the annual taxes paid. This is to encourage the use of the non-congested rural highway network. In this instance the term average passenger car is misleading. The more typical vehicle is likely to be a jeep, station wagon or light truck used not only for consumption purposes (sightseeing, trips to the beach, etc.) but also as an input into agriculture. The variable maintenance costs caused by these vehicles and their technical operating coefficients (fuel consumption, depreciation, etc.) are, however, close enough to that of the average passenger vehicle to permit considering them in the same category.

Seven-ton truck. The effect of imposing a system of economic user charges upon trucks is in general to lower taxes paid by heavy vehicles. Only in Honduras would it mean an increase for diesel powered trucks. It is easy to see from the level of existing taxes why only a few gasoline powered vehicles of this class are found in Central America. In most of the countries the tax paid by the gasoline powered truck is more than twice that paid by the equivalent diesel truck. There is no reason why the two fuel types should be treated differently. In the adjustment process illustrated above the gasoline tax is never quite reduced (with the exception of Nicaragua) to the level of five cents a gallon, the amount required to equate the two fuel taxes. This could be done by lowering the gasoline tax at different rates in those countries having a higher initial gasoline tax. For these large trucks some differential tax between fuel types will have only a minor impact on the choice of vehicle used mainly because of the substantial comparative advantage of diesel. For smaller trucks where there is a greater degree of substitution, the difference is more critical.

The adjustment process outlined above is somewhat more abrupt than that for passenger vehicles. At the same time the transition is easier, as it usually means a decline in the total tax burden. The higher rates for diesel trucks in the first year in Nicaragua and Costa Rica are the result of the substantial increase in the fuel tax and the reduction of only 20 percent in import duties, which for both these countries currently account for most of the taxes on this type of vehicle. The tax in the early years is thus really the capital loss and not an actual cash outlay.

165

The figures for heavy vehicles assume that they use only uncongested highways. For most of these vehicles this is a good approximation. Some vehicles do, however, use the city streets and thus should be subject to the same system of congestion charges as paid by passenger vehicles.[9] Trucks making urban deliveries during congested hours should carry a license similar to that of the passenger vehicle. This would encourage the delivery of goods during uncongested periods (early morning and late evening) and thus lead to a more efficient utilization of urban streets.[10]

Collection costs

It has not been possible to accurately assess the costs of administering the proposed system of user charges. There appears to be no reason why these costs should be excessive. The fuel taxes can be administered in much the same manner as at present. Fuel taxes are collected at a central point (the refinery) with relatively little administrative machinery required. The differential fuel tax by region of sale should impose no additional burdens on this system other than the necessity of adding one more figure to the invoices of products moving out of the refinery.[11] The costs of the licensing system in urban areas should not be high if reliance is placed upon the use of existing retail outlets. The retail margin would then be determined competitively. Costs of enforcement can be kept to a minimum if the appropriate level of penalties are applied (see page 139).

The costs of administering the current system are largely unknown but are probably a small fraction of revenues collected. There are no reasons why the proposed system of two simple taxes should change this.

Revenues and the implementation process

The transition process illustrated above is meant to provide only the broadest guidelines for the direction of change. There are no reasons why the timing of the various steps cannot be changed. Experience with congestion levies will in particular dictate the pace of change. Regardless of the implementation process, care should always be taken to insure that the specified fiscal goals

---

[9] Charges could possibly be higher per vehicle kilometer as large vehicles take up more space and have slower rates of acceleration.

[10] This is already done to some extent. The private costs of congestion are high enough to encourage deliveries in off-peak periods.

[11] A simple administrative system would be to require the signature of retailers on invoices to which the lower tax rate applies. Once the destination has been confirmed this can be checked against tank capacity, number of vehicles in the area, etc. To mitigate the differentials between nearby outlets, more than two rates of tax may be used in several concentric zones.

are taken into account and that the changes in the tax burden do not induce avoidable taxpayer hostility or political difficulties.

There are also no reasons why the process of implementation cannot vary considerably between countries. The process illustrated above does not attempt an absolute equality in all taxes. Congestion costs may differ substantially from city to city and this should be reflected in the price. Cost conditions for non-congested travel are roughly similar for all countries; therefore, the economic user charge should be the same. Differences in fuel taxes, however, are not likely to alter the pattern of transport. It is quite possible to have a gas tax of 12 cents per gallon in Guatemala and 8 cents per gallon in Honduras and still have a negligible effect upon total transport costs. Close cooperation between the countries of the common market would be desirable but is not absolutely necessary for the implementation of the proposed system of user charges. Nevertheless the context of the common market does provide an opportunity for "harmonization" of motor taxation.

The Common Market

The desire of the Central American countries to work toward the formation of a common market has certain implications for the pricing of road services.[12] In general it requires that pricing policies be roughly similar. At present little difference exists in the taxation of road services from one country to another. In moving toward a more efficient system of pricing for road services some differences could exist without seriously impeding or distorting the pattern of trade between countries. Most of the use of highways is at present for domestic trade, and variances in user charges will be reflected only indirectly in the relative efficiency of one country versus the other—that is, in the terms of trade. The existence of a common market with a greater degree of factor mobility than normally exists in international trade does, however, provide some incentives for any one country to maintain the same degree of efficiency (or inefficiency) in its pricing of road services as the rest of the countries of the common market.

If one country should change unilaterally to a more efficient system of pricing (such as the one recommended in this study) it should improve the efficiency of the domestic economy. An adverse movement in the terms of trade with other members of the common market could occur—the lowering of user charges can be considered equivalent to a unilateral lowering of tariffs. This should not, however, be exaggerated; improvements in domestic efficiency should by far outweigh any adverse movement in the terms of trade and the

---

[12] For a discussion of the problems of transportation in a common market see ECC, *Options in Transport Tariff Policy*, Brussels, 1965.

167

net impact will be improvement in the welfare position of all members of the common market. Some pressure will be generated for the remaining countries to follow suit since countries tend to place considerable emphasis on their export position. Improvements in domestic efficiency should make exports cheaper and thus improve the relative position of the country with respect to the other members of the market.

Neither the change in the terms of trade nor the improvement in domestic efficiency are likely to be of sufficient magnitude to require the complete harmonization of the system of user charges in the common market for purposes of economic efficiency.[13] The system of taxes proposed by this study does in fact make more attractive the use of road taxes for general revenue purposes. The system is primarily a local one in that most of the revenues come from the urban areas. If the demand for urban street services is relatively inelastic one city could raise more revenues than those forthcoming from the congestion charge without having to worry about the level of charges in other cities. This study has not emphasized this possibility because of the existence of better alternative sources of tax revenues.

International trucking

One of the major difficulties in the attempts of the European Common Market to reach an agreement concerning road user charges has been over the impact it would have on the carrying trade. In the European case complications exist in the form of competing modes of transport, particularly railroads, inland waterways, and pipelines. Countries that have relied primarily on rail transport have been reluctant to adopt a system of user charges that would favor the development of highway transport.[14] In the Central American Common Market the difficulties associated with competing modes of transports are of little importance. The predominance of the highway in carrying common market trade is an established fact. The difficulties occur over who does the carrying. The tendency has been to restrict the domestic carrying trade to domestic carriers and to make minimal concessions on the international trade.

The current system of user charges strongly favors the registration of vehicles to be used in international trade in Honduras. Here trucks pay no purchase taxes and are subject only to a nominal license fee (more or less the system recommended by this study). Since all the countries permit vehicles

---

[13] Other than, perhaps, for purposes of avoiding discrimination in the carrying trade. See below.

[14] Enforced in many cases by restrictive regulation of the highway transport industry. France is probably the best example here.

registered in another state to move goods in and out of their country, the expectations would be that vehicles registered in Honduras would quickly dominate this trade. This does not seem to have occurred.[15] There are several reasons for this. Present restrictions on domestic carriage tend to favor the registration of vehicles in one of the countries engaged in the trade. A vehicle registered in El Salvador can pick up goods in Guatemala, cross the border into El Salvador and pick up and discharge goods in its movements throughout El Salvador. A vehicle of Honduran registry could pick up goods in Guatemala and discharge in El Salvador but it could only pick up goods destined for a third country. This disadvantage may be sufficient to offset the lower fees paid for Honduran registry.[16] Additional reasons can be found in the preference of local producers for local transport firms and in discriminatory border practices. The more likely reason is that international trade is still relatively small when compared to domestic trade and trucks engaged in the crossing of borders do so only as a small part of their domestic carrying.

As trade between common market countries expands the incentives will be greater for specialized firms to enter the industry and to concentrate on carrying only the international trade. The system of user charges proposed by this study would prevent the dominance of the international carrying trade by the vehicles of any one country. Transport firms would have no incentives for establishing in one country rather than another.[17] Each country would have approximately the same fuel tax and negligible license fees and import duties. If this is not done the protectionist reflex of most of the countries is likely to lead to further restrictive measures on international trade in order to prevent Honduras from becoming the dominant carrier of the common market. This, of course, would increase the costs of not lowering the user charges in non-congested areas. The total costs of not doing this may be quite high if the alternative is greater restriction of international trade.

Restrictive practices

At present all of the countries of Central America carry out various restrictive practices that are an implicit indirect tax burden on road users and at the same time are incompatible with the concept of a common market. The most

---

[15] However the casual observations of the study team suggest that the number of Honduran vehicles on international routes is somewhat disproportionate to the relative importance of Honduras in this trade, but there are no statistics that would permit the making of a better judgment.

[16] A 7-ton diesel truck pays nearly $600 per year in license fees and import duties in El Salvador versus the $75 charged in Honduras.

[17] Except for valid economic reasons such as the lower cost of factors of production.

important of these restrictive practices are the unnecessarily complicated border crossing procedures (see p. 37). These could be eliminated at a small cost (more customs officials, longer hours of operation, etc.) and would encourage the greater use of the largely uncongested road network linking the countries. This study strongly recommends that steps be immediately undertaken to correct this problem. The necessary studies have been undertaken by SIECA (The Common Market Secretariat) and only require implementation.

Other restrictive practices that affect road users are those associated with fuel refining and tire production. Both these industries are singularly inappropriate for import substitution. Other than in Nicaragua (and possibly in Costa Rica) the costs of domestic fuel refining have been largely offset by lowered crude margins.[18] Steps should be taken, however, in some countries to rationalize the internal price structure. The maintenance of the pre-refinery price structure in Costa Rica and Nicaragua does not make economic sense and should be taken into account in making adjustments in the fuel taxes. Restrictive retailing practices such as in Guatemala also impose an unnecessary burden on the road users.

A full study of the problems of the tire industry is beyond the scope of this study. However, the implications for road users cost and therefore for road user charges of the establishment of further productive capacity and a failure to rationalize the output of the two existing firms should be borne in mind.

Congestion Charges in the Cities

The most significant departure of the proposed system from the existing system of user charges is the use of congestion levies in the urban areas. The use of congestion levies to control the growing traffic problems of the urban areas throughout the world is not a new idea but is a concept that has been widely discussed over a considerable period of time by economists and engineers.[19] There appears to be a general consensus that these charges are both

---

[18] Care should be taken in considering the expansion of this industry, particularly if at some later stage it should become a supplier for the petrochemical industry.

[19] See, for example, G. Roth, *Paying for Roads: The Economics of Traffic Congestion*, Middlesex, Penguin, 1967. J. W. Gibbons, and A. Porter "Economic Costs of Traffic Congestion," *Highway Research Board Bulletin* 86, 1954. H. Greenberg, "An Analysis of Traffic Flow," *Operations Research*, 1959, pp. 79–85. C. A. Rothrock, "Urban Congestion Index Principles," *Highway Research Board Bulletin* 86, 1954, pp. 26–39. A. A. Walters, "The Theory and Measurement of Private and Social Cost of Highway Congestion," *Econometrica*, 1961, pp. 676–99.

feasible and desirable. Yet in spite of this long standing interest there are very few examples of their application. Even the few examples that do exist tend to be only accidentally associated with the congestion problem rather than the result of a conscious effort to price property for the use of road space.

Why the reluctance to impose these charges? Part of the answer lies in the natural reluctance of society to change its past pattern of behavior. Urban congestion of today's magnitudes is relatively new and some lag is to be expected between the conception and implementation of new ideas. Perhaps also the emphasis that has been given by many economists to the desirability of revenues collected from road users approximating the costs (however defined) associated with the construction of roads has led to the lack of public understanding about the nature of road services and the economics behind the rationing of these services. In the urban areas where this rationing has become more and more of an acute problem, the costs of ignoring the economics of resource allocation are increasing with great rapidity.

The general recommendations made concerning urban congestion charges are applicable to most of the cities of the world, particularly those of the more developed countries. It is possible though that the efforts to bring the problem under control could be first attempted by the developing countries. They do not have as great a commitment to the unrestricted use of the private automobile nor do they have the resources to waste on relatively extravagant solutions such as freeways and subways. The introduction of congestion charges in Central American cities could thus be a pathbreaking step towards the solution of an almost universal problem.

The level of congestion

The recommendations of this study have stressed the gradual movement towards an adequate level of congestion charges. Just what is an adequate level is difficult to define. The estimates of congestion charges made have been based on the existing urban street system. An alternative to congestion is, of course, to improve facilities through greater investment. The political possibilities for doing this would increase if large amounts were raised through congestion charges, particularly if these sums were earmarked for expenditures within the urban areas.

The decision to invest should be based on a comparison of benefits and costs, however, and not taken merely because the necessary funds are available. The benefit, for example, of increasing speed from 10 kph to 15 kph on a given street could be achieved by the cost of adding an additional lane of traffic. If the benefits exceed the cost this would be an economic investment. On the other hand, the investment costs associated with increasing traffic speed to 30 kph may be prohibitive. It is a question of balance; it is unlikely that it will ever be economic to eliminate congestion completely. Some degree of congestion, especially if controlled by appropriate charges, is always likely to be the cheaper alternative to increased investment. In the Central American cities where investment in urban streets has long been neglected it is likely that there are substantial investment opportunities. The paving of the streets of Tegucigalpa is a good example.

A program to introduce congestion charges should take into account the lower levels of congestion that may result from increased investment. The levels of congestion charges suggested by this study have for this reason purposely been on the low side. The gradual introduction of these charges will allow time to establish at least what could be regarded as tolerable levels of congestion and possibly a fairly close approximation to the most economical level where a balance is maintained between congestion costs and the reduction in traffic volume. Even at the economically most efficient levels of congestion, revenues are likely to be substantial. A possible tolerable level of congestion is one in which traffic moves at speeds of 15 kph. This would require a charge of 9 cents a vehicle kilometer, a much higher levy than that used to estimate the revenues from congestion charges on pages 158–160. If this speed is to be achieved, most Central American cities will require a marked slowing down of the growth of traffic density and/or a very large-scale investment program.

Earmarking

The large revenues which most likely could be generated through congestion charges raise the question of what should be done with these resources. There are no economic reasons why these revenues should be tied to expenditures on urban streets. As was suggested above, fairly high levels of congestion on urban streets are always likely to be economic, and the earmarking of revenues from congestion charges to street improvements may then lead to uneconomic investments.[20] The case for earmarking must be made on other grounds. It may be the only way of getting political acceptance of the system of congestion charges. It is quite conceivable that the danger of over-investing in urban streets is quite remote in Central America, but such schemes tend to develop their own internal pressures for continuance and the expediency of today could become the disaster of tomorrow. It could be dangerous to develop in urban motorists the feeling that they somehow have the "right" to spend the revenues from charges which are imposed to ration scarce space. At the very least there should be a contribution to general revenues equivalent to a rental for the area given over to streets, and comparable to the ground rent chargeable on adjacent land.

---

[20] It should be obvious that there is no economic rationale for linking these revenues to non-urban road expenditures.

It would thus be preferable to avoid any earmarking of these funds. A possible maximum concession to political needs might be to associate part of the funds with urban street maintenance. A sum equivalent to *x* dollars per kilometer of street could be transferred to a separate maintenance budget. This would appeal to the urban motorist and at the same time introduce some stability into the maintenance program.

The main suggestion with respect to these funds is that they be used to provide municipal governments with a much needed source of general revenues. The deteriorating quality of local government requires that a new revenue base be established and congestion charges may help fill this gap.

Summary

The preoccupation of this study has been the efficient allocation of resources. It is therefore focused on the problem of economic productivity—or simply how to get the most out of the natural endowments of the economy. To achieve this requires some restructuring of the current system of user charges employed in Central America. In general charges should be lowered in rural areas and raised in urban areas. The simplest instruments for achieving this are urban license duties and general fuel taxes. Resource allocation need not be the only concern of the policy-maker. Other goals such as the redistribution of income or raising of public revenues can also be encompassed within the framework outlined. Both of these policy aims have been accorded a minor role, first because no precise policy guidelines have been established by the Central American governments and second because road user charges are not necessarily the most efficient way of accomplishing either of these goals.

There is no doubt that some income redistribution will occur through changes in the amount and pattern of road user charges but to or from whom and in what amounts is difficult to judge. Use of roads and the benefits obtained are widespread and indirect so that such a redistribution is not to be condemned out of hand as inequitable. A major exception is the charge for the use of passenger cars in congested areas; this would impinge largely on middle and upper income classes and thus could well be pushed considerably above the level of marginal costs on distributional grounds. It is probably better, however, to concentrate initially on achieving an efficient allocation of resources through road user charges and leave the problem of income distribution (if it exists) to other means.

Additional government revenues may be raised by user taxes. The recommendations regarding the implementation of the change to a system of economic user charges have kept certain revenue goals in mind. In general it should be possible to increase revenues by a modest amount in each year of the transition without resort to taxes other than those required to cover

173

variable maintenance plus congestion costs. Should additional revenues be required taxation of road users offer some possibilities, but these can only be judged in the light of the alternative sources of taxation. In view of these other alternatives (land taxes, income taxes, excise taxes, etc.) and because of the complexities it would introduce into the common market relationship, only a weak case can be made for using taxes related to the use of roads as a revenue source. A better source of revenue would be the taxation of some of the benefits resulting from road construction or improvements. In many instances these can be readily identified through changes in property values. This suggests that some form of betterment taxes accompany road improvements. In urban areas where property identification is adequate this could take the form of a simple tax per meter of frontage on the road.[21] In rural areas where property identification is much harder excise taxes or export taxes on farm output could be substituted for the property tax. In most of the Central American countries a tax on coffee exports would be the best way to pay for road improvements in coffee areas. Most of the benefits occur to the coffee producers and the supply curve of coffee has the advantage of being fairly inelastic. In any case these are matters more closely related to general tax and fiscal policy rather than transport policy.

Aside from the recommendations directly concerning road user charges, this study has suggested that a number of steps be taken that are of a more general nature but which are related to the efficiency of transport. Of primary importance is the elimination of excessive border crossing costs. The high costs of border crossing are an unnecessary burden upon common market trade in addition to being wasteful per se. Other recommendations have stressed the elimination of the inefficiencies that result from excessive control and protection of the transport industry and associated inputs.

One final point that needs considerable emphasis concerns the collection of data. If rational economic decisions are to be made care must be taken in providing the data necessary to make these decisions. Too often in Central America there is a tendency to collect statistics without any obvious reason. This haphazard collection of data can be expensive and of limited use. The governments concerned should carefully review their data needs and take steps to insure that these needs are adequately filled. The best way to collect data is to know what it can be used for and it is hoped that this Study will provide some guidelines. Of obvious importance are statistics on traffic movements, maintenance costs by type of road, vehicle speeds, freight rates, etc. Most of these can be collected for very little cost and would be of much use in formulating policy for the pricing and construction of roads.

---

[21] This type of tax is currently being considered for the city of San Salvador.

SELECTED BIBLIOGRAPHY

Books

De Weille, J. *Quantification of Road User Savings.* World Bank Staff Occasional Paper Number 2. Baltimore: The Johns Hopkins Press, 1966.
Roth, G. *Paying for Roads: The Economics of Traffic Congestion.* Middlesex: Penguin, 1967.
Van der Tak, H. G., and de Weille, J. *Reappraisal of a Road Project in Iran.* World Bank Staff Occasional Paper Number 7. Baltimore: The Johns Hopkins Press, 1969.
Walters, A. A. *The Economy of Road User Charges.* World Bank Staff Occasional Paper Number 5. Baltimore: The Johns Hopkins Press, 1968.

Articles

Dick, A. C. "Speed-Flow Relationship Within an Urban Area." *Traffic Engineering and Control,* October 1960.
Gibbons, J. W., and Porter, A. "Economic Costs of Traffic Congestion." *Highway Research Board Bulletin 86,* 1954.
Goss, R. O. "Economic Appraisal of Port Investment." *Journal of Transport Economics and Policy,* September 1957.
Greenburg, H. "An Analysis of Traffic Flow." *Operations Research,* 1959.
Lipsey, R. G., and Lancaster, Kelvin. "The General Theory of the Second Best." *Review of Economics and Statistics,* 24 (1955–56).
Rothrock, C. A., and Keefer, L. E. "Traffic Speeds and Volume Measurement." *Highway Research Board Bulletin 156,* 1956.
————. "Urban Congestion Index Principles." *Highway Research Board Bulletin 86,* 1954.
Soberman, Richard M. "Economic Analysis of Highway Design in Developing Countries." *Highway Record* [Highway Research Board], No. 115, Publication 1337, 1966.
Sutarwala, Z. K., and Mann, L. "A Formula for the Allocation of Maintenance Funds for Highways Using a Mathematical Model to Predict Maintenance Costs." *Engineering Experiment Station Bulletin No. 72.* Baton Rouge: Louisiana State University, 1963.
Walters, A. A. "The Theory and Measurement of Private and Social Costs of Highway Congestion." *Econometrica,* 1961.

Reports

Adley Associates Inc. *Technical Report, Transportation Study.* El Salvador: Ministerio de Obras Publicas, Direccion de Urbanismo y Arquitectura, 1968.
British Road Research Laboratory, East Africa Transport Planning Research Unit. "A Study of Road Maintenance Costs in Kenya." Mimeograph, 1966
EEC. "Options in Transport Tariff Policy." Brussels, 1965.
Estudio de Velocidades en las Carreteras de Costa Rica. San Jose, 1964.
IBRD Report No. TO–584a. "Appraisal of the Western Highway Paving Project, Honduras." 1967.
IBRD Report No. WH–170a. "Economic Development and Prospects in Central America." June 5, 1967.

National Research Council. "The AASHO Road Test." Publication No. 816.
   Washington, D.C., 1961.
Primero y Segundo Censo Nacional Agropecuario, 1950 and 1965/66.
Report of the Committee on Road Pricing (The Smeed Report), Appendix 2.
   London: H.M.S.O., 1965.
Research on Road Traffic. London: H.M.S.O., 1965.